Pray
for
Friends
and
Enemies

Praying
for
Friends
and
Enemies

JANE E. VENNARD

Augsburg

MINNEAPOLIS

PRAYING FOR FRIENDS AND ENEMIES

Scripture quotations are from the New Revised Standard Version Bible, copyright © 1989 Division of Christian Education of the National Council of the Churches of Christ in the United States of America. Used by permission.

Cover image copyright © 2001 Tony Stone Images. Used by permission.
Cover design by Timothy W. Larson
Book design by Timothy W. Larson

Library of Congress Cataloging-in-Publication Data
Vennard, Jane E. (Jane Elizabeth), 1940–
  Praying for friends and enemies / Jane E. Vennard.
    p. cm.
  Includes bibliographical references.
  ISBN 0-8066-2769-7 (pbk.)
    1. Intercessory prayer—Christianity. I. Title.
BV215.V46 1995
248.3'2—dc20   95-3487
                                                       CIP

The paper used in this publication meets the minimum requirements of American National Standards for Information Services—Permanence of Paper for Printed Library Materials, ANSI Z329.48-1984.

Manufactured in the U.S.A.   AF 9-2769

05   04   03   02   01   1   2   3   4   5   6   7   8   9   10

In memory of my parents

John K. Vennard
1909–1969

Dorothy Walton Vennard
1908–1993

Contents

Acknowledgments

My thanks to:

BETH GAEDE, my editor, whose intuition led her to invite me to write this book before we ever met. She has been a clear, respectful, and wise companion in the creative process.

KAREN HANSEN, my research assistant, who tracked down everything in print having to do with intercessory prayer.

CATHIE WOEHL, my secretary, for her good humor and for her computer.

THE REVEREND TOM ESSELMAN, C.M., my spiritual director, who helped me write from the heart of prayer.

CHRIS WERNER, my dance teacher, who guided the rhythms of my creative process.

SWANEE HUNT, who provided the cabin at her Columbine Ranch, where much of this book was written. And to Barb and Al Reynolds, the ranch caretakers, who know the fine art of providing hospitality while respecting solitude.

THE PASTORS AND PEOPLE of Sixth Avenue United Church of Christ and Capitol Heights Presbyterian Church, who shared stories, questioned my assumptions, and prayed with me while I wrote.

ST. ANDREWS UNITED METHODIST CHURCH, for giving me the opportunity to share my work in progress.

Acknowledgments

THE REVEREND NORA SMITH, the Reverend John Lee, the Reverend Alta Smith, the Reverend David Grishaw-Jones, and the Reverend Mark Meeks, who listened, shared ideas, made connections, and opened closed doors.

TRISH DUNN, Carolyn Earley, Barbara Flanigan, and Margaret Johnson, who helped me say no to the book I didn't want to write and yes to the one I did.

MY STUDENTS AND DIRECTEES, whose prayerful lives have given me questions to ponder, insights that startle, and stories to tell.

MY HUSBAND, JIM LAURIE, whose support, encouragement, and comfort are a mainstay of my creative process and life.

JAMIE AND PAUL, my stepsons, who keep me from taking myself too seriously.

Introduction

PRAYING FOR FRIENDS AND ENEMIES is intercessory prayer. In intercessory prayer we pray on behalf of others. We ask not for ourselves but for them. We ask God to intercede in human affairs, making God's presence known on earth. Many of the psalms are cries of intercession:

> *Give justice to the weak and the orphan;*
> *Maintain the right of the lowly and the destitute.*
> *Rescue the weak and the needy;*
> *Deliver them from the hand of the wicked.*
> (Psalm 82:3-4)

We all are familiar with prayers of intercession, and we offer them up quite frequently. We pray for the safety of our children. We pray that a friend's pain might be eased. We pray for the welfare of our country. We pray that the victims of earthquakes be saved. Sometimes we pray more specifically, asking God for exact outcomes: "God, grant Sam that scholarship." "God, put Sarah's cancer into remission." "Please, God, my husband needs that job he applied for today."

Groups as well as individuals ask God to intercede in worldly affairs. People in worship on Sundays pray for members and ask God to bring more people into their community of faith. People in cities gather, often in interfaith groups, to ask God in the languages of many different religions to stop the violence that plagues the streets. People gather regularly throughout the world to pray for people; others pray for the protection of mother earth.

In intercessory prayer, as in all forms of prayer, God is the initiator. God calls us into relationship, and prayer is our response. Although many of us do not pray regularly and often let this primary relationship with God slide to the edge of our attention, we are all pray-ers. In moments of distress we call out instinctively for help. In moments of blessing we say, "Thank God!" From the depth of our human relationships and our love for creation, we cry out to God for others.

Intercessory prayer is only one form of prayer. No one form is more important than another, for all forms of prayer bring us more fully into right relationship with God. This book is designed not to "teach" you intercessory prayer but to lead you deeper into the intercessory prayer life you already have. Because prayers of all forms are different avenues toward God, the exploration of one form of prayer has the possibility of expanding all forms of prayer. Intercessory prayer is the starting place of this exploration. Who knows where the spirit might lead.

When I was a child hiking in the Sierra Nevada, my father taught me to hunt for cairns, small piles of rocks left by other hikers to show the way across granite slopes and through open meadows. (My father was from New England, and I have since learned that these markers are called "ducks" in the west.) I remember the experience of feeling utterly lost and disoriented and the great relief of spotting those few rocks, placed carefully by human hands to let me know others had passed this way.

Paul's prayer for the Ephesians will serve as the cairns for our journey. It serves to raise questions, point to experiences, and lead us deeper into our relationship with God.

> I do not cease to give thanks for you as I remember you in my prayers. I pray that the God of our Lord Jesus Christ, the Father of glory, may give you a spirit of wisdom and revelation as you come to know him, so that, with the eyes of your heart enlightened, you may know what is the hope to which he has called you. . . . (Ephesians 1:16-18)

Paul addresses his prayer to "the God of our Lord Jesus Christ." So we will begin our exploration of intercessory prayer by asking, Who is God, not only for Paul, but for us? How do we understand and experience the God of Jesus? Jesus taught us that God is a god of love, as close to us as an *abba* (Hebrew for "father," or even "papa"). Jesus told us that God is so near that even the hairs of our heads are all counted (Luke 12:7). How are we to address this God in our prayers of intercession?

In addition to pointing us to God, Paul's prayer urges us to look more deeply into ourselves. We know Paul to be a man of great faith, and a man who experienced doubts and contradictions that he confessed to the Romans: "I can will what is right, but I cannot do it. For I do not do the good I want, but the evil I do not want is what I do" (Romans 7:18-19).

We also know Paul is a man of action, as well as a man of prayer. Paul is working tirelessly to lead people into relationship with God, and this relationship is what he prays for. Paul prays that God will open the hearts and minds and eyes of the Ephesians so that they will know God.

Our knowledge of Paul invites us to ask who we are. We are created in the image of God, yet we are filled with human fears and limitations. In chapter 2 we ask: What is our relationship with God like? What are our doubts and inconsistencies? How congruent are our prayers and our actions? Paul's prayer invites us to explore our images of God, our responsibility to God, and our responsibility to those for whom we pray.

Paul did not know Jesus alive. He only met him as the risen Christ. Like Paul, we only have the Gospel stories to help us understand Jesus' life on earth. In these stories Jesus tells his disciples to intercede for the lost (Matthew 9:36-38), and he tells his followers to pray for their enemies (Matthew 5:44). Jesus practices intercessory prayer when he prays for Peter (Luke 22:31-32), when he prays for his disciples (John 17), and in his final hours when he prays: "Father forgive them, they know not what they do" (Luke 23:24). These passages and other Gospel stories of people interceding for their loved ones—perhaps stories Paul knew himself—can deepen our understanding of intercessory prayer. We will examine several key passages from the Gospels in chapter 3.

Before Paul prays to God, he greets the Ephesians with the words "I do not cease to give thanks for you. . . ." We assume that Paul has affection for these people for whom he prays. What of the people we do not hold in high regard? What of those who oppress us, who have done us wrong? Jesus taught us to love our enemies. What might happen if we were to bring those people into our prayers? Do they have something to teach us? That will be the challenge we will address in chapter 4.

In his intercessory prayer Paul does not ask God to persuade, seduce, demand, or threaten the Ephesians. He does not ask God to make them *do* anything in particular. Paul's words do not indicate any hidden agendas. His prayer is open ended, for when the Ephesians receive the spirit of wisdom, the enlightened heart, and the knowledge of hope, Paul does not know what they will do, how they will behave, or who they will be. Paul responds to God in prayer, then he leaves the outcome to God. In chapter 5 we will think about what led Paul to pray in this manner and ask, Are there situations where more specific outcomes need to be prayed for? How willing are we to "let go and let God"?

After Paul's greeting and prayer for the Ephesians, he goes on to instruct them in rules for a new life. We do not know if the prayer opened the Ephesians' hearts and minds and eyes, either of individual women and men or of the community as a whole. Paul prayed, wrote his advice, and sent the letter off. Did it have any effect? In our technological world we want to know outcomes, statistics, results. Are we willing to follow Paul's example and pray for others, even when we do not know what the effect will be? And even more intriguing, are we willing to enter into intercessory prayer when we do not know what the effect will be on us, the pray-ers? By entering into prayer for others, we might be the ones who are transformed. These questions shape the discussion in chapter 6.

Questions, not answers, are the heart of this book. As we circle around the questions, we begin to form understandings, only to be led to further questions. We will draw on the experiences of many in addition to Paul who have gone before and left us cairns for the journey. At the end of each chapter you will find suggestions for ways to delve more fully into the questions and explore the markers that have been discovered. To help you continue the journey and explore more questions, the final chapter will include some specific ways we might deepen our practice of intercessory prayer.

Practice is a useful word, for it implies an ongoing process and excuses us from ever having to give a performance. We are never supposed to master prayer. We are never given a final exam. We will not be asked to show our skill. We are simply invited to continue to practice. And we will forget. Like the young child who finds a million ways to not practice the piano, we will interrupt our practice of prayer. But Father Thomas Keating, teacher of centering prayer, reassures us that faithfulness in prayer is simply the willingness always to start over.

God calls us to this faithfulness. God calls us into prayer. But we do not have to depend on our will alone. God is near. Even when we forget to pray, disbelieve, or give up, God sends the Holy Spirit to our assistance.

> For we do not know how to pray as we ought, but that very
> Spirit intercedes with sighs too deep for words. (Romans 8:26)

ONE ❦ The Theology of Intercessory Prayer

I Am Who I Am.
—Exodus 3:14

G OD CALLS US INTO RELATIONSHIP. God is love. God is as close to us as an abba. These are assumptions about God that help us pray. When we hold these assumptions and attitudes, we are willing to respond to God in prayer because we trust God and believe we are loved unconditionally. We know that growing closer and closer to God through prayer leads us to become more loving toward ourselves and our sisters and brothers. We welcome the intimacy with God to which we are called.

OUR ASSUMPTIONS ABOUT GOD

These assumptions of God's goodness and closeness might not be your assumptions. You might hold different images of God. Maybe you were taught that God is a judge, ready to pronounce you guilty whenever you make a mistake. Maybe you were taught that God is distant, watching the struggles of creation without caring or entering in. Maybe you were taught that God is close to us but as a spy rather than a sustainer, waiting to catch you doing something wrong rather than reaching out to support you.

I heard about a little girl who held such a negative image of God, not because her parents had taught it to her but because she had misunderstood the words of Scripture. Her family had often prayed Psalm 23 together, and the images of poetry became very real to her. But they did not comfort her as the family intended, for what this child heard in verse 6 was not the reassurance that goodness and mercy would be hers all the days of her life. She thought "Shirley Goodness" and "Mercy" were the names of two old ladies, sent by God to follow her and spy on her forever. She was terrified!

Our assumptions about God profoundly affect our response to God. Remember how you felt when you were a student and were assigned to a teacher with a reputation for being harsh and critical and emotionally distant. You might have tried to get the class assignment changed so that you would not have to relate to that teacher. If you had to attend that class, you might have entered the room afraid, hugging your books close in a protective stance. Maybe you were watchful and wary and as silent as could be. You probably never looked up to meet this teacher's eyes, for when you did you saw hostility and contempt.

Or you might have entered this teacher's class unafraid and ready to "take the teacher on." In this case you might have been aggressive and hostile. You probably talked back, challenging the teacher's authority, trying to prove the teacher wrong. Maybe you looked the teacher directly in the eyes and returned the disdain you saw reflected there.

Whichever behavior you chose, you did so in response to the reputation of the teacher. Your assumptions about that teacher, garnered from other students who had gone before, made you belligerent or frightened, silent or sarcastic. Based on our personal makeup, background, and prior experiences, we will each respond differently to a teacher who is a tyrant, but the reputation of that teacher will profoundly influence our individual responses.

Now remember the experience of being assigned to a teacher with a reputation for fairness, good humor, a love of teaching, and respect for students. Most likely your response was different. Maybe you approached the class eagerly with a lightness in your step and anticipation in your heart. You probably greeted the teacher when you walked in. You might have seen your excitement mirrored in the teacher's face. Maybe you decided to test this teacher to see if he or she was really as good humored and fair and you had been told. Maybe you talked back or pushed the limits to see how the teacher would react. As the teacher responded consistently with love, you probably realized that your assumptions about the class were valid. You began to relax and trust. You started to learn.

We do not change gods like we can change teachers. But we can change our assumptions and our attitudes about God. We can overcome old teachings about God that no longer fit our experience. We can read about other people's understanding and experience of God. We can look at our own responses to God and ask ourselves on what assumptions they are based. We can test the validity of our assumptions through different forms of prayer.

God calls us into relationship but does not demand instant intimacy. As in human relationships, love grows slowly as trust develops. God waits while we deal with our fears and our doubts and our curiosity. God waits while we test our assumptions. God loves us while we take all the time we need to return that love. We must examine our assumptions and attitudes, for they, not God, determine our response to God.

GOD'S GOODNESS AND POWER

Intercessory prayer, asking God to intercede in human affairs, invites us to question our assumptions about God's power, love, and proximity to us. Intercessory prayer forces us to confront the greatest challenge to our faith: why does God allow suffering if God is good and God is close? Suffering makes some people assume that God is distant and does not care, or that God sends suffering to judge the wicked, or that God is good but powerless.

Rabbi Harold Kushner, author of *When Bad Things Happen to Good People*, wrestles with issues of suffering and God's power. He shares his emerging belief that God is all good but not all-powerful.[1] This does not mean that God is powerless. Rather it means that there are some things God cannot do. One of the things that God cannot do is change the laws of nature. If the engines on an airplane stop in mid-flight and the airplane is pulled to earth, God cannot reverse the laws of gravity and raise the airplane up.

Another thing that God cannot do is change what has already happened. When I have sent a manuscript to be considered for publication and the editor sends me a response by mail, I might breathe a prayer when I see the envelope: "Please, God, make this a letter of acceptance." God can do nothing about this letter, for the editorial staff has read the article and already made a decision. The letter is simply a confirmation of that decision. God cannot rewrite the past.

In addition, God cannot interfere in humankind's freedom of choice. If God had the power to make us always choose good, suffering might be eliminated. But we would become puppets with no will and no voice of our own. Without the power to participate in shaping our own lives, we would not reflect the image of God. God is the creator of the universe, and women and men, made in God's image, are called to be creative as well. Creativity is impossible without freedom.

Limited in power, God is still not powerless, for God has the power to love and be a companion to those who are searching, struggling, and suffering. God might not be able to reverse the plunge of the airplane, but God can bring comfort to those on board and to the relatives of those who die. God cannot make the letter one of acceptance, but God can help me deal with rejection and give me the will to rewrite the article, send it elsewhere, or begin again with a new idea. God cannot make us choose good, but God can open our minds to discover options. God can soften our hearts as we recognize the consequences of our actions, not only for ourselves but for others and for all of creation.

God is close and God is loving. God is not all-powerful. God is intimately involved in human affairs, but God does not fix what is wrong. Rabbi Kushner tells a story of a little boy who goes out on an errand for his mother. He is gone much longer than his mother expects. When he returns she asks him what took him so long. "I stopped to help Tommy," the child replies. "His bicycle was broken." His mother said she did not know that he could fix bicycles. "Oh, I didn't help him fix it," he responded. "I helped him cry."[2]

Rabbi Kushner's theology and understanding of prayer come from examining individual suffering caused by illness, accident, and misfortune. Walter Wink, professor at Auburn Theological Seminary, explores God and prayer in relation to the suffering caused by the Powers, which he understands to be the structures and institutions that exploit and oppress and perpetuate injustice in the world.[3] Professor Wink's theology expands Rabbi Kushner's assumptions about God.

Professor Wink assumes God is good because of the promise that God has made to creation. Throughout Scripture God has promised a world of justice where all will have food and care and opportunity, where neighbor will treat neighbor with respect, where no one will oppress another. In the New Testament this promise of harmony is called the "reign of God."

Professor Wink also assumes God is powerful. He sees God's power in God's ability to heal and believes that all healing is of God.[4] As he understands it, God's will is that all people are free to become everything God created them to be, and that when this happens the fulfillment is of God. Professor Wink also assumes that God is close and involved in creation, and that when we pray for peace and justice and liberation, God hears our prayers. But

> God's ability to intervene . . . is sometimes tragically restricted in ways we cannot pretend to understand. It takes considerable spiritual maturity to live in the tension between these two facts: God has heard our prayer, and the Powers are blocking God's response.[5]

God's power is limited by the Powers, but this is no reason not to pray. Rather the existence of the Powers calls us to pray more fervently, for "intercession is spiritual defiance of what is, in the name of what God has promised."[6] Because we look around and see that God's promise has not yet been fulfilled, we must become engaged with God in God's struggle for justice. Intercessory prayer is the first step.

When we become involved in intercessory prayer, we become part of the "politics of hope."[7] Hope sees a new future. Hope believes this new future into being. Hope leads to action, which creates the new future. "In our intercessions, we fix our wills on the divine possibility latent in the present moment, and then find ourselves caught up in the whirlwind of God's struggle to actualize it."[8]

Both Harold Kushner and Walter Wink come to the conclusion that God is all loving, God is engaged in human struggle , and God hears our prayers. They both conclude that God is powerful but not *all-powerful*. This assumption is often disturbing to people who were brought up to believe that God is omnipotent. An omnipotent God makes us feel safer, more dependent, less responsible. We can relax when an all-powerful God is in charge.

GOD'S IMMUTABILITY

The immutability of God is another assumption that must be examined if we are to enter faithfully into intercessory prayer. Saying God is immutable means that God is absolute and cannot be changed. With so many changes in our lives, assuming God is stable can be very reassuring. In the hymn "Immortal, Invisible, God Only Wise," these words appear in stanza 3:

> *We blossom and flourish like leaves on the tree*
> *Then wither and perish; but naught changeth thee.*[9]

Intercessory prayer certainly changes the one whom is prayed for and the one who offers the prayer, as we will explore in depth in chapter 6. But does prayer change God? And if God is not immutable, what new assumptions must we make about the nature of God?

Scripture is full of references to God being moved by human events to change God's mind. In Genesis 18, Abraham convinces God not to destroy all the people of Sodom after God had declared the town's total destruction. Moses begs God: "Change your mind and do not bring disaster on your people" (Exodus 32:12). In the book of Jonah, the people of Nineveh change their sinful behavior, and we read:

> When God saw what they did, how they turned from their evil ways, God changed his mind about the calamity that he had said he would bring upon them; and he did not do it. (Jonah 3:10)

In the New Testament the parable of the friend at midnight tells us that through perseverance in prayer God's decision might be changed. The householder denies the friend's request for bread, explaining that "the door has already been locked, and my children are with me in bed; I cannot get up and give you anything" (Luke 11:7). But after continual knocking the friend is given everything he needs.

Jesus changes his mind in his encounter with the Canaanite woman in Matthew 15:21-28. First he denies her request that he heal her daughter. When she argues with him, he listens and then says: "'Woman, great is your faith! Let it be done for you as you wish.' And her daughter was healed instantly" (v. 28).

Revelation 8:1-5 tells us that the prayers of people mingled with the incense of the angels change the course of history.

> And the smoke of the incense, with the prayers of the saints, rose before God from the hand of the angel. Then the angel took the censer and filled it with fire from the altar and threw it on the earth; and there were peals of thunder, rumblings, flashes of lightning, and an earthquake. (vv. 4-5)

Walter Wink comments on this change of events:

> Human beings have intervened in the heavenly liturgy. The uninterrupted flow of consequences is dammed for a moment. New alternatives become feasible. The unexpected becomes suddenly possible because people on earth have invoked heaven, the home of the possible, and have been heard. What happens next happens because people prayed.[10]

If God can be changed by human supplication, is nothing absolute? God's love is absolute and unwavering. God's will to create justice is constant. Through the words of the prophets of Hebrew Scripture and through the birth and life and death of Jesus, God has promised a better world in which all things are made new. In intercession we call out to hold God to that promise. In the words of philosopher Douglas Steere: "We must not conceive of intercessory prayer as an overcoming of God's reluctance but as a laying hold of God's highest willing."[11] God's love, God's will, and God's promise are immutable, but the way these are expressed and enacted might vary. Intercession might cause a change of plan.

GOD'S NEED FOR US

The change of plan might have to do with the interdependence of God and humankind. When we pray we offer ourselves to God. We become agents of God's acts in new ways because we pray. By entering into intercessory prayer, we give God opportunities that God did not have before. As more people open themselves to God in prayer, God has more possibilities for responding to our needs. If God is to intercede in human affairs, if God is to continue to bring the creative power of love and justice into our lives, God needs us to pray and to act.

One Sunday in adult education I suggested to the class that God might need us. A participant responded vehemently against the idea. "I can't stand the idea of God needing me," she cried. "Everyone in my life seems to need me or need something from me. I need God to carry me through. If God needs me . . . Oh! It's just too much!"

This might be your response to the idea that God has need of us. But reflect on this image a little more closely. When need is all one-sided in human relationships, trust and intimacy are slow to develop. When need is mutual, and giving and receiving are balanced, love can grow. The image of God needing us makes God more accessible for a close and compassionate relationship. Just as

God is ready to weep with us when the broken cannot be fixed, so must we be ready to weep with God, who hears our prayers but cannot respond.

God's need for our intercessory prayer is recorded in Scripture. The prophet Isaiah describes the Lord God crying out: "I looked, but there was no helper; I stared, but there was no one to sustain me . . ." (Isaiah 63:5). He also tells of the Lord's displeasure when "he saw that there was no one, and was appalled that there was no one to intervene . . ." (Isaiah 59:16).

The prophet Ezekiel, speaking the word of the Lord, recounts the sins of Israel in chapter 22, telling of the profanity, the evil, and the injustice of the people. Through the mouth of Ezekiel, the Lord ends his condemnation with these words:

> And I sought for anyone among them who would repair the
> wall and stand in the breach before me on behalf of the land,
> so that I would not destroy it; but I found no one. (v. 30)

God calls us into relationship. When we respond to the call, we are meeting God's need as well as our own. God needs intercessors. God is appalled when no one appears, bereft when no one steps forward. Intercessory prayer begins with a loving, compassionate God who is committed to justice and who needs us to be present and active in the creation of the future. How are we to respond to God's need?

FOR REFLECTION AND DISCUSSION

1. As you read this book, be aware of the assumptions about God that are being made. Feel free to disagree, argue, and talk back as a way of clarifying your own assumptions and attitudes about God.

2. How do you respond to the idea that God might not be all-powerful? Think of experiences that might have had a different outcome if God were omnipotent.

3. What aspects of God do you believe to be absolute? What aspects are changeable? How do these assumptions influence your intercessory prayer life?

4. What is your experience of friendship based on mutual need? Can you take your understanding gained in human relationships into your assumptions about God? What does it mean in your life if you believe God has need of you?

5. Are the assumptions you hold today about God the same as those you held ten, twenty, or thirty years ago? How have your attitudes and assumptions and images changed?

ACTIVITIES

1. Make a list of your assumptions about God. Reflect on the questions these assumptions raise, as well as the answers they provide.

2. Are you able to hold the tension between God hearing your prayers and God being unable to respond? Are you praying for something right now in your life to which God is not responding? Write a brief description of this experience of tension.

3. Look for other stories in Scripture, besides the ones mentioned in this chapter, that tell about God changing as a result of human behavior.

TWO ❦

Human Responsibility

God created humankind in God's image.
—Genesis 1:27

GOD NEEDS US. God loves us unconditionally. We are the beloved daughters and sons of God. God weeps with us in our pain. God delights in our job. God suffers with the oppressed and the abused. God celebrates when justice is restored, when the lost are found, when peace comes to a people. God calls us into a relationship of mutuality, where we are needed as well as loved. God calls us into relationship not only with God but with our sisters and brothers and all of creation. And to be faithful people of God, we must intercede for others, not only in prayer but in action as well.

In Isaiah 42:5-7, the prophet presents us with an image of how we are loved and needed:

> *Thus says God, the Lord,*
> *who created the heavens and stretched them out,*
> *who spread out the earth and what comes from it,*
> *who gives breath to the people upon it*
> *and spirit to those who walk in it:*
> *I am the Lord, I have called you in righteousness,*
> *I have taken you by the hand and kept you;*
> *I have given you as a covenant to the people,*
> *a light to the nations,*
> *to open the eyes that are blind,*
> *to bring out the prisoners from the dungeon,*
> *from the prison those who sit in darkness.*

According to the research of feminist theologian Virginia Mollenkott, the one called to do the Lord's work, the righteous servant of God, has been traditionally understood by Jewish scholars to be the personification of the Hebrew nation.[1] Christian scholars have traditionally understood the servant to be Jesus the Christ. She suggests that both of these traditional understandings of Isaiah's righteous servant of God are too narrow. She believes Isaiah's call is to all of us to become God's servants. We are the ones to whom God has given breath. We are the ones whom God has called, taken by the hand, and kept. We are the ones who are to be a covenant to the people and a light to the nations. We are the ones who are to free the people in bondage.

OUR IMAGES OF OURSELVES

This call to be God's righteous servants brings us face-to-face with the images we hold of ourselves. We might see ourselves as unable to respond or unworthy of the call. We might assume God is calling everyone else but us. We might begin to wonder how this call will affect our lives. We might worry that we will have to change and give up our familiar ways of living. The call might hold to our faces a mirror in which we see our arrogance. We might imagine we are the only chosen, or the first chosen, better than others, more capable of doing God's work. We might believe all of the above at once! God's call leads us into the complexity of our self-images. We must begin to explore who we are before we respond to God's call to servanthood.

Self-examination is not only a psychological issue. It is a theological issue as well. Theologian Carl Rahner believes that God and humanity are so intimate that "the personal history of the experience of God signifies, over and above itself, the personal history of the experience of the self," and "the personal history of the experience of the self is the personal history of the experience of God."[2] Created in God's image as we are, belonging to God as we do, the exploration of God and the exploration of ourselves cannot be separated. Just as we cannot experience who we are apart from our gender, our race, or our place in history, we cannot experience ourselves apart from God.

As we explore ourselves in relation to God and God's need of us, we might feel overwhelmed, particularly if we remember that Jesus teaches us to "be perfect . . . as your heavenly Father is perfect" (Matthew 5:48). But many scholars believe that a more accurate translation of the Greek word translated "perfect" here would be "whole" or "complete." The word *perfect* conjures up images of consistent holiness, goodness, and purity. The word *whole* allows for contradictions, inconsistencies, and mistakes.

When we explore the wholeness of God through images, we find many contradictions: God the loving Abba, God the angry judge, God the vulnerable babe, God the mother hen. We read about God being loving and angry and forgiving. We hear of God's power and of God's need. We know God as the Father, as the Son, and as the Holy Spirit. God is rich and complex and multifaceted. And we are made in God's image.

If we are willing to be honest in the exploration of ourselves, we will find many contradictions in our makeup. We know ourselves as strong, responsible adults, and at the same time we know ourselves to be wounded children. We might be hardworking at one time and lazy another, courageous in one moment and terrified and immobilized the next. For every act of kindness, there might be an unkind act. Every time we criticize ourselves for our impatience, we might look for other moments when we have been patient. We are inconsistent, complex, and rich in nature. And we are in good company.

Peter pledges to be faithful to Jesus unto death (Mark 14:27-31), and then denies him three times (Mark 14:66-72). Paul confesses to the Romans, "I can will what is right but I cannot do it" (Romans 7:18). German theologian Dietrich Bonhoeffer, imprisoned and executed by the Nazis during World War II, writes from his prison cell that he struggles with his experience of self.[3]

Bonhoeffer asks himself, Who am I? and responds at first with how others see him: calm, cheerful, friendly, proud, equable, and smiling. He then tells what he knows of himself: he is restless, longing, like a bird in a cage. He writes about his fear and his anger and his thirst for words of kindness. He confesses to being weary and empty at prayer. He writes:

> *Who am I? This or the other?*
> *Am I one person today, and tomorrow another?*
> *Am I both at once? A hypocrite before others,*
> *And before myself a contemptibly woebegone weakling?*[4]

Who among us has not struggled with these questions in far less trying circumstances? Someone tells us they appreciate our calm presence, but we know we are seething with anger inside. Another mentions our compassion, when we are well aware of our judgments of others. A friend thanks us for the way we listened to her, and we have already forgotten what she said.

God does not call us to perfection or consistency. God calls us into partnership. Created human in God's image, we are called into the deepest sense of our own humanity. God calls us to be righteous servants in the world, to enter into the struggle for justice through prayer and action. God's call illuminates our limitations, our doubts, and our fears as well as our longing to serve, our unique gifts, and our compassionate hearts. We do not completely figure out who we are before we accept God's call. We respond to the call from the midst of the struggle for self-understanding, as Bonhoeffer did:

> *Who am I? They mock me, these lonely questions of mine.*
> *Whoever I am, thou knowest, O God, I am thine.*[5]

OUR PLACE IN COMMUNITY

As our experience of self cannot be separated from our experience of God, our experience of self cannot be separated from our experience of neighbor. Children learn about themselves in their families of origin—their earliest neighbors. They learn more about themselves as they move out into their neighborhood and into their schools. They continue to learn about themselves in the context of their many communities. Community shapes the images we hold of ourselves.

In community we discover that we share with our neighbors many longings and needs, delights and hope, even as we explore how different we are from one another. We discover our unique gifts and the gifts of others. We learn to give and to receive. We learn about friendship and enemies, conflict and cooperation, equality and oppression. In community we discover that the one to whom we pray is not only *my* God but *our* God.

We do not enter an exclusive relationship when we respond to God's call to partnership. We enter into a relationship with all God's people, who are also responding to God's need for intercessors. Belonging to God is to belong *with* our sisters and brothers and all of creation. Being in relationship makes us part of a huge web where friends and enemies, leaders and followers, neighbors near and far are brought into relationship. As a part of this web we discover that

> What we need at heart is no different from the need of our neighbor and our world, and . . . we know we can never get what we need alone or apart from our neighbor's crying and groaning. For what we need is not the salvation of our own soul but the new heaven and the new earth, the reign and the rule of God.[6]

God calls communities, as well as individuals, to become righteous servants of God. When a community raises its collective voice in supplication to God, the community experiences a power that surpasses individuals praying alone in their rooms. A whole church prays together for healing in a family that is torn by tragedy. People cross religious boundaries to come together in a citywide memorial service for those who have died of AIDS and to pray for an end to this tragic disease. Small churches come together in the inner city to pray for the homeless and the chronically mentally ill.

Collective voices raised in intercessory prayer are no more likely to be heard by God than one small voice crying in the wilderness. The power of prayer in community is the relationship

that is strengthened among neighbors and the energy that is garnered to do God's saving work in the world. When we know that
others share with us the suffering of broken families, the anguish
of those with HIV and AIDS, the hopelessness of the poor or the
mentally ill, we are not so overwhelmed with God's need for us to
free all those who sit in darkness. God has not called us to a task
and then abandoned us. God is with us and we are with each other.

ACTING IN COMMUNITY

Sometimes intercessory prayer in community helps individuals recognize their particular gifts for doing justice in the world. When I
was in seminary, intercessory prayers offered during worship
would range over all the injustices in the world. Opportunities to
serve abounded. Candlelight vigils were announced, marches for
causes of justice were organized, work trips to Central America,
the Middle East, and South Africa were planned. If we could not
attend these activities, we were encouraged to give financial support. God's need and the needs of our sisters and brothers became
overwhelming.

Anne, a fellow student and close friend, confessed to me one
day that she was feeling constantly guilty. "It doesn't matter how
much I do," she said, "there is still so much to be done. And everyone thinks their issue is the most important. When I decline an
invitation to participate, I feel like I have let the whole world
down, but I can't take on literacy, AIDS, and abused women in
addition to what I am already doing." Her words were a great
relief to me, for I was feeling much the same, and some of my guilt
was in response to Anne's work in Central America.

Anne was fluent in Spanish and very knowledgeable about the
political, economic, and social issues of the region. She took regular work trips to be of service and hoped for a ministry there when
she graduated. When I listened to her speak about the people and
the issues, and saw her eyes light with love, compassion, and a
fierce passion for justice, I would think, "I should be doing that.
Her work is so worthwhile, so necessary, so important." Then I

would begin to doubt myself, thinking I was lazy, afraid of the hardship, or lacking in compassion. I would compare my work to hers, and my efforts toward justice would come up lacking. I had told her none of this.

When Anne shared her guilt with me, I was able to tell her about mine. As I let it all pour out, she listened, then began to smile, and finally broke into laughter. I was a little taken aback when she laughed at my confession, but trusting her as I did, I knew she had discovered something important. "I can't believe it!" she cried. "All year I have been watching you become so involved in women's issues—writing, speaking, leading, organizing. I felt so ashamed that I was not working with you. I felt like I had abandoned you."

Our confessions, our discussion, our friendship helped us acknowledge our passions, our gifts, and our limitations. We recognized that our different work served the same God of justice. We let go of comparison and self-recrimination. We made a commitment to pray for each other and for the work we were doing. We both felt energized and empowered. "I'm so glad this is settled," Anne said with a smile. "You take care of women. I'll take care of Central America. What a relief."

Becoming the righteous servant of God is a sacred responsibility to be shared with sisters and brothers. Trying to do all the work or trying to do any piece of work alone does not honor God's call to community. Thee are many ways to share the work. Anne and I chose separate spheres and supported each other with prayers. One small church has formed a committee to support a member who is working in Mexico to bring literacy to a village. They send supplies and care packages, love and prayers, and keep the whole church community aware of progress and needs. Another small congregation looked at all the needs of their community and picked one activity to do together. Every Saturday a group from the congregation serves a meal at one of the homeless shelters. Over a few months all who are able participate, and those who cannot physically go support the activity with contributions, encouragement, and prayers.

To become servants of God, we must search our hearts to discover our gifts and our limitations. We must trust our neighbors to do the same. For God's work is the responsibility of all God's children. Division of labor allows us to be faithful to God's call to relationship and community. Paul teaches us:

> Now there are varieties of gifts, but the same Spirit; and there are varieties of services, but the same Lord; and there are varieties of activities, but it is the same God who activates all of them in everyone. To each is given the manifestation of the Spirit for the common good. (1 Corinthians 12:4-7)

THE PRAYER-ACTION CYCLE

God needs intercessors. God needs us. We are the righteous servants of God. Sometimes our intercession will take the form of prayer. Sometimes our intercession will take the form of action. One will always lead to the other in a cyclical process. As our commitment to intercession grows, we will discover a congruence in our actions. When we pray for peace, we will act for peace. We might be unable to take specific action for peacemaking half a world away, but we can translate that distant need into a nearby need and become a peacemaker in our communities, our churches, our families, or our hearts. When we pray for the starving children of the world, we will open our eyes to the physical, emotional, and spiritual hunger of children closer by and take responsibility for feeding some of those children in some way.

Congruence of word and deed, prayer and action, are part of the responsibility of becoming servants of God. Congruence is so important to Episcopal bishop John Selby Spong that he says, "If we are not willing to live it, then let our lips be mute and our tongues be silent whenever we kneel to pray."[7] Recognizing the inconsistencies of our humanity, I prefer the gentle and encouraging words of St. Thomas Moore, who prays, "The things, good Lord, that we pray for, give us the grace to labor for."[8]

FOR REFLECTION AND DISCUSSION

1. Reflect on ways your family of origin and your early communities shaped the self-images you hold today. What communities are shaping your self-images now?

2. How does the image of servanthood fit with your other images? How do you wish to respond to God's need of you?

3. In what ways are you already acting as God's righteous servant? What are your ways of bringing justice to the world?

4. How congruent are your prayers and action? Are there ways you could bring your prayers and your actions closer together?

ACTIVITY

Make a list of the many ways you can respond to the question Who are you? Include roles you play (teacher, volunteer, writer), relationships (sister, brother, wife), feelings (happy, sad, angry), qualities (creative, shy, pessimistic), and images or metaphors (a mother bear, a child of God, a storm cloud). Keep adding to your list, finding as many ways as possible to answer the question. Go back over your list, noticing contradictions, surprises, and patterns in your responses. How does your list speak to you about wholeness?

THREE ✒ *Gospel Stories of Intercession*

> *Jesus saw their faith.*
> —Mark 2:5

J ESUS WAS A MAN OF PROFOUND FAITH. Jesus honored his relationship with his Abba through prayer. Jesus taught us about prayer by example. He practiced prayer. He lived prayer.

Jesus gave us no specific instructions regarding intercessory prayer, although he did tell his disciples to pray for the lost (Matthew 9:36-38), and he told his followers to pray for their enemies (Matthew 5:44). We also have examples of his practice of intercession when he prays for Peter (Luke 22:31-32), when he prays for his disciples (John 17), and when he prays in his final hours for those who have condemned him to death (Luke 23:34). We can also assume that much of Jesus' private time with God was spent in intercessory prayer, for praying for others was an integral part of the Jewish religion.

INTERCESSION IN HEBREW SCRIPTURE

From the beginning of their history, the leaders and prophets of the people of Israel prayed for their nation. They acted as intercessors by virtue of their offices.[1] The people of Israel recognized the power of intercession and begged their leaders: "Do not cease to cry out to the Lord our God for us . . ." (1 Samuel 7:8). Moses, reluctantly leading the people from captivity in Egypt through the wilderness to the promised land, constantly called out to God for the deliverance of the people. He cried out for food when the people hungered. He cried out for mercy when the people strayed:

> O Lord, why does your wrath burn hot against your people, whom you brought out of the land of Egypt with great power and with a mighty hand? . . . Turn from your fierce wrath; change your mind and do not bring disaster on your people. (Exodus 32:11-12)

Samuel reveals the importance of intercessory prayer when he says, "Far be it from me that I should sin against the Lord by ceasing to pray for you . . ." (1 Samuel 12:23). Daniel enters into a long and passionate plea for forgiveness and mercy for the people of Israel, who have sinned and brought suffering and destruction upon themselves and shame upon holy Jerusalem:

> Lord, let your face shine upon your desolated sanctuary. Incline your ear, O my God, and hear. Open your eyes and look at our desolation and the city that bears your name. . . . O Lord, hear; O Lord, forgive; O Lord, listen and act and do not delay! (Daniel 9:17-19)

In Hebrew Scripture the leaders and the prophets and the priests, because of their official positions, were the ones to intercede for the people. Jesus honors that history of intercession but removes it from the few and offers it to the many. "He enlarged its range, revealed its immense possibilities, and made it . . . a fundamental practice in the lives of all his followers."[2]

PAUL'S INTERCESSIONS

Paul followed Jesus' example and practiced intercessory prayer. Prayers for the early Christian communities, as well as requests for prayer, are found throughout his letters. We read, for example, "I appeal to you, brothers and sisters, by our Lord Jesus Christ and by the love of the Spirit, to join me in earnest prayer to God on my behalf . . ." (Romans 15:30).

Paul's letters show us that intercession was vital in the prayer life of the early Christian communities.[3] Paul's letters extend to us Jesus' invitation to make intercession a fundamental practice of prayer.

CHRIST THE INTERCESSOR

Throughout the history of the early church, and for Christians who pray today, the presence of the living Christ has deeply informed our prayer. For many Christ is the intercessor. Through his death and resurrection he stands before God in eternity, making constant intercession for us.

> The very fact of our Lord Christ standing before the face of God is an act undertaken for us, is an intercession in action .... In this mystery we see the heights of intercessory prayer, that at its most perfect expression it is a state, a state of standing before God for a purpose connected with creation; it is an offering of a life and of a will, a pleading.[4]

As Christ stands before the face of God interceding for us, he also intercedes in us and through us. Christ activates our longing to respond to God's call to relationship. And our intercessory prayer invites and allows Christ's redeeming work to be done in the world through us. "He is the giver, we the channel used by him to carry the gift."[5]

Flora Wuellner, clergywoman and author of several books on prayer, has a slightly different image of Christ the intercessor. She places Christ beside us as we pray for others. We are there "not as healers, not as channels, but as beloved companions of the Healer, helping to focus and intensify the presence of the Christ."[6] Christ supports, encourages, and teaches us as we appeal to God on behalf of others. We are led by Christ to stand before God and before all creation, offering our prayers for the fulfillment of God's promise.

INTERCEDING WITH JESUS

In Gospel times people went directly to Jesus when a loved one was in need. They knew Jesus as one who carried God's healing power in the world. When they went to Jesus on behalf of another, they were practicing intercessory prayer. These stories of faith can teach us about the power of prayer. They can help us trust the goodness of God.

Two of these stories tell about parents interceding for their children. One was a father named Jairus, a leader of the synagogue who fell to his knees before Jesus. Jairus told Jesus that his daughter had just died and implored Jesus to come and lay hands upon her so that she would live (Matthew 9:18). The other was a mother, a Canaanite woman, who shouted out to Jesus, begging him to heal her daughter who was tormented by a demon (Matthew 15:22).

When our children are at risk, our prayers of intercession are passionate and profound. Parents want to keep their children safe and healthy and alive. When human efforts fail, parents turn with great force and longing to God, as did these two parents in Matthew's Gospel. Their passionate pleas moved Jesus to action but in very different ways.

Jesus responded to Jairus by immediately accompanying him to his home, where he put out the mourners and raised the young girl from her bed. Jesus does not respond so immediately to the Canaanite woman. The disciples find fault with her for her continual shouting. Jesus tells her that he was sent only to serve the house of Israel. But she will not give up her beseeching. She falls to her knees, and after Jesus refuses her again, she offers one more argument, which he cannot deny:

> He answered, "It is not fair to take the children's food and throw it to the dogs." She said, "Yes, Lord, yet even the dogs eat the crumbs that fall from their masters' table." (Matthew 15:26-27)

Jesus hears the Canaanite woman's argument, praises her faith, and changes his mind. Jesus heals her daughter instantly.

Both of these stories attest to the healing power of God in human lives. They underscore the faith of the petitioner. They teach us that when we have a deep desire and longing to help another, one prayer might not be enough. To be faithful in prayer is to keep on praying. When our children's very lives are at risk, how can we do otherwise?

AN UNEXPECTED ANSWER

The story of Lazarus and his sisters Martha and Mary (John 11: 1-44) gives us another example of intercession. When Lazarus fell ill Mary and Martha sent word to Jesus: "Lord, he whom you love is ill" (v. 3). Jesus, believing that the illness was not serious, did not respond immediately but stayed two days longer where he was. When he finally arrived at the home of Mary and Martha, Lazarus had died and had already been in the tomb four days.

Martha and Mary's request had not been answered. They were sad, disappointed, and probably angry with Jesus for not coming when he was called. Martha left her house and went to meet Jesus on the road, saying to him, "Lord, if you had been here, my brother would not have died" (v. 21). One sister complained, the other wept, but both sisters experienced the pain of unanswered prayer.

Jesus was greatly disturbed by the sisters' grief and joined them in their weeping (v. 35). He then went to the tomb, ordered the stone removed, and called to Lazarus to come out. Lazarus emerged, still bound by the burial clothes, and Jesus said, "Unbind him, and let him go" (v. 44). Mary and Martha's brother was restored to them through the love of Jesus. The sisters' prayers were answered in a totally unexpected way.

Mary and Martha have much to teach us about intercessory prayer. They called out to Jesus for the sake of their brother. They knew what they wanted when they sent word. They wanted Jesus to come immediately and to heal Lazarus. When this did not happen, they did not turn away from Jesus, but each in her own way stayed in relationship with him. Then Jesus intervened in a manner that the women had not imagined. They were surprised by the answer to their prayers. Mary and Martha teach us to ask for what we want, to speak from our hearts when we do not receive the hoped for response, and to open ourselves to the possibility of God's unexpected intervention in our lives. Mary and Martha help us to know the process of intercessory prayer.

INTERCEDING BY ACTING

In the first two stories reviewed above, the parents go to Jesus to intercede for their daughters. In the Lazarus story the sisters call Jesus to come to them. In the story of the four friends (Mark 2: 1-12), the paralytic is carried into the presence of Jesus. This intercessory prayer is both silent and active. The friends do not speak to Jesus; they make no request. They simply and with great difficulty place their friend at the feet of Jesus.

This story teaches us that sometimes intercessory prayer is very hard and that we might not be able to do it alone. One person could not have carried the paralyzed person into the presence of Jesus. This action had to be a group effort. When the four friends arrived at the house where Jesus was teaching, they realized they could not enter through the door, for the crowds were so large that the entrance was blocked. But they did not give up. They looked for another way. They climbed to the roof of the house, dug through it, and lowered their friend into the presence of Jesus.

Jesus saw their faith and proceeded to heal their friend. The faith that Jesus saw consisted of love of neighbor, commitment to action, and trust that Jesus would do for their friend what was best. These four intercessors did not beg, they did not speak their desire. They looked for no specific outcome. They offered their friend to Jesus and let go.

Taking action is a form of intercessory prayer. Rabbi Abraham Heschel, who marched with Martin Luther King Jr. in Selma,

Alabama, in 1965, was heard to say, "I feel like my feet are praying." Our hands pray when we help to build a house for Habitat for Humanity. Our eyes pray when we read to the blind. Our ears pray when we listen with compassion to the struggles of another. Our arms pray when we embrace and hold a grieving friend.

A couple in my church regularly bring their friend who uses a wheelchair to worship. Every Sunday they go to get him, do the hard work of lifting and assisting, and carry him into the presence of God in community. One Sunday their car broke down, but they persevered and all three arrived in time for communion and the fellowship of those gathered in praise and prayer. The four friends we read about in the Gospel of Mark are present today in this couple and in all people who act with love, commitment, and solidarity for those in need.

Reading scripture with our ears tuned to intercessory prayer can offer us new insights for our own practice of prayer. Priests and prophets, outcasts and high-ranking officials, men and women pray for others. They pray persistently and passionately. They pray silently. They pray through action. These people plead, argue, complain, and weep. They pray for mercy, for justice, for healing, for hope. Listening to these faithful people encourages us to follow in their footsteps. As we pray for others, we are blessed by those who have gone before.

FOR REFLECTION AND DISCUSSION

1. How does the Jesus of history and the Christ of faith guide you and support you in intercessory prayer?

2. When you enter into intercessory prayer, imagine the Christ beside you supporting and encouraging you. Does this make a difference in your experience of prayer?

3. Remember a time when you felt like the Canaanite woman, pleading for mercy, arguing with God, and trying to convince God to do as you wished. What happened as a result of that difficult time? What did the experience teach you about intercessory prayer?

4. When you believe your prayers have not been answered, are you more like Martha who complained or more like Mary who wept?

5. Remember a time when you were surprised by an answer to prayer, when you received something you had not expected. How has that affected your faith?

ACTIVITY

Paul requested that the Christian community in Rome pray for him. We occasionally ask others to pray for us. Sometimes people are praying for us without our asking. To explore the experience of receiving the prayers of others, enter into the following meditation.

Settle yourself in a comfortable position and enter into prayer with a few words of praise, petition, or gratitude. Quiet your mind, and open your heart to the experience of the paralytic.

Imagine that you are a resident of Capernaum and know that Jesus has come to teach. Imagine the paralysis in your arms and legs and head. Experience the despair . . . the isolation . . . the hopelessness . . . as you hear others running to be with Jesus.

Imagine your four friends arriving and gathering around you. Imagine yourself being lifted . . . carried. Imagine what goes through your mind and your heart as you realize you are being carried toward Jesus. Hear the crowds. Feel the bumps as your friends get jostled. Realize that they cannot get you to the door. Imagine what it feels like to be lifted and pushed . . . then left to lie on the roof while your friends do the hard work of digging. Imagine how you are feeling about your four friends at this moment.

Imagine yourself being lifted once again and lowered into the room where Jesus is teaching. See the love in your friends' eyes. See Jesus look up at them in surprise. Imagine his gaze returning to you. Hear his words: "Your sins are forgiven." Take in these words of forgiveness and hold them in your heart. Imagine the words penetrating your numbness and your pain.

Imagine Jesus returning to you. Imagine him saying, "I say to you, stand up and take your mat and go to your home." Let these words resonate in your body . . . feelings . . . and mind. Imagine your limbs coming slowly to life. Imagine getting up . . . picking up your mat . . . and starting for home.

Imagine the people as they part to let you through. Imagine their questions . . . their silence. Imagine what it feels like to be upright . . . moving. Imagine a prayer of thanksgiving forming in your heart. Know that you will need the rest of your life to ponder the full meaning of this miracle.

Take a few deep breaths. Let the imagery fade. Slowly return your attention to the room in which you are sitting. Offer a brief prayer of thanksgiving. (You might wish to write about your experience in your journal.)

FOUR 🦅

Intercession for Enemies

Pray for those who persecute you.
—*Matthew 5:44*

A NUMBER OF YEARS AGO I was complaining to a friend about a person whose behavior was aggravating me. Margaret listening, asking for details, clucking in sympathy, I talked about my feelings of being violated, misunderstood. I talked about the phone calls, the hostile words, the irresponsibility. There was no doubt when I finished my tale that lines had been drawn and I was dealing with an enemy.

I felt such relief at having poured out my anger and hurt and sadness to such a compassionate heart. We sat in silence for a moment. Then Margaret said, "I will pray for you in this difficult time." I felt comforted by her willingness to take me into prayer and experienced a new peace about the situation. And then Margaret added, "I will also pray for her."

My heart lurched, my head reeled, tears welled up in my eyes. I felt betrayed. Margaret was *my* friend. I wanted all her prayers. I wanted nothing for my nemesis. She didn't deserve attention or kindness or prayers. I was right; she was wrong. I wanted to preserve the cloak of righteousness I had wrapped around myself.

I knew that if I let Margaret's willingness to pray for my enemy touch my heart, I would no longer be able to hold on to my anger and self-pity. I would have to move into a new relationship with this woman and with God.

I was so far from praying for the one who persecuted me that I wanted no one else to pray for her either. I wanted her cut off from me, from Margaret, and from God. I wanted to be right, with God on my side. Margaret's kind and gentle words, "I will pray for her as well," pulled the rug out from under me and I was forced to look at where I stood.

DIFFICULT WORDS

The invitation to pray for our enemies is disorienting, although we have heard the words of Jesus many times: "But I say to you, Love your enemies and pray for those who persecute you" (Matthew 5:44). These words are easy if we simply read them. They become difficult when we attempt to obey them. For to pray for our enemies is to bring them before God. When I bring them before God, I am reminded that they too are loved by God. Then I must recognize that the one I am holding at arm's length is my sister or my brother.

Another reason it is difficult for us to pray for those who persecute us is that when we do, we are forced to see that the enemy is within us, as well as without. The woman I was so angry at mirrored aspects of myself that I did not wish to see. In my self-righteousness I could say smugly: "I'd never behave that way." But the truth is, I knew I could behave as she did—because I had. All things come clear before God, so praying for others reveals to us what we have been trying to hide from ourselves.

When we experience others as enemies, we harden our hearts against them. We do this for our own protection, for survival. We close down to keep ourselves safe. But when we pray for those who have hurt us, our hearts soften and we begin to feel compassion. We become vulnerable. We feel at risk. Therefore, we must move slowly and gently when we begin to pray for our enemies.

Prayers for those who persecute us begin with what is in our hearts. If I am filled with fury, I need to express it. If I am afraid, I need to cry out my fear. If I would like to see my enemy removed from the face of the earth, I need to give voice to that desire. By praying this way, I remain safe with God at my side. This sense of safety is often necessary when we are preparing to take the first step in praying for enemies. The opening, the vulnerability will come later.

THE PSALMIST'S CRIES

The psalms give us examples of beautiful, poetic prayers cried by people who wanted relief from persecution, vengeance against evil, and action by a God of justice. The Hebrew people cried out to God against their enemies:

> *O my God, make them like whirling dust,*
>   *like chaff before the wind.*
> *as fire consumes the forest,*
>   *as the flame sets the mountains ablaze,*
> *so pursue them with your tempest*
>   *and terrify them with your hurricane.*
> *Fill their faces with shame,*
>   *so that they may seek your name, O Lord.*
> *Let them be put to shame and dismayed forever;*
>   *let them perish in disgrace.* (Psalm 83:13-17)

Although these words are filled with rage, notice the phrase of reconciliation amidst the call for destruction: "so that they may seek your name, O Lord."

The purpose of this intercessory prayer is not only to give voice to what is in the psalmist's heart and to call down God's fury on the enemy. The purpose of the prayer is also to bring the enemy back into relationship with God. But in order for the angry Hebrews to move toward reconciliation and hope, the heart of rage has to be expressed.

Sometimes the evil that has been done is so great and the hurt and the pain so deep that when the wounded one cries out to God, there are no words of hope, only words of revenge and despair. Psalm 137 is an example of such an experience. As the Israelites lament over the destruction of Jerusalem, they weep; they vow not to sing in the foreign land to which they have been exiled; and they take pledges to remember Jerusalem. Then they recall the day of Jerusalem's fall and how the enemy shouted to tear down the walls to the foundation. In the anguish of exile and memory they cry out:

> *O daughter of Babylon, you devastator!*
>   *Happy shall they be who pay you back*
>   *what you have done to us!*
> *Happy shall they be who take your little ones*
>   *and dash them against the rock!* (Psalm 137:8-9)

What are we to make of such desire for violence, such total despair? Bonhoeffer wrote that the expression of these horrifying thoughts shifts the desire for vengeance to God alone.[1] Turning our deepest and most destructive desires over to God is an act of trust that God will ultimately vindicate the just in God's own time. The graphic images, as terrible as they are to imagine, are so deep and so real and so specific that they free us from having to take personal revenge. When we speak of the unspeakable, we need not act.

Psalm 137 leaves the reader with no words of comfort or reconciliation or assurance that justice will be done. But history reassures us. After many years of exile, Jerusalem was restored, and the Hebrew people returned home to the center of their religion and their culture. Justice was done in God's way and in God's time.

DOUBTING GOD'S PRESENCE

Starting to pray where our hearts are, rather than where we think they ought to be, brings us closer to God. Sometimes when we are in a rage and are feeling persecuted by another, we doubt God's presence. We wonder how this terrible thing could be happening if God loves us. Our own faith is shaken when we experience injustice.

A young pastor called me in great despair over the treatment he had been receiving from a person in authority. Phone calls were not being returned, meetings were being held without the pastor, financial difficulties were not being addressed. This situation had been going on for some time, and David felt betrayed, abused, and hopeless. He was so angry he could not talk straight. When he paused in his tale of woe, I asked him what his prayers had been like during this time.

"Prayers?" he responded. "What prayers? I can't pray. I don't know where God is. I feel abandoned. How could God let this happen? How can God's servants be so incompetent? I'm so angry! So angry! I'm angry with God!"

"Tell God how angry you are, David. Take your fury into prayer. God can handle it. Pray the psalms, David. Let them guide you," I responded.

When we need to turn to God in despair, Psalm 22 can ease the way:

> *My God, my God, why have you forsaken me?*
> *Why are you so far from helping me,*
> *from the words of my groaning?*
> *O my God, I cry by day, but you do not answer;*
> *and by night, but find no rest.* (Psalm 22:1-2)

When we feel like my friend David felt, not only can we not begin to think of praying for our enemies, we cannot pray at all. First we need to return to God, we need to feel God's love, we need to open our hearts to God. By praying about our experience of abandonment, we move back into relationship with God. We begin to respond again to God's loving invitation. We answer God with anger and despair, but we answer. And when we answer, we discover God has been there all along.

Yet it was you who took me from the womb;
you kept me safe on my mother's breast.
On you I was cast from my birth,
and since my mother bore me
you have been my God.
Do not be far from me,
for trouble is near
and there is no one to help. (vv. 9-11)

GUIDANCE FROM THE PSALMS

When we are being persecuted, the psalms guide us in giving voice to our desire for revenge. They help us pray our anger toward God about the experience of abandonment. The psalms also teach us about cries for deliverance and protection when we feel like the world is falling in on us.

Deliver me from my enemies, O my God;
protect me from those who rise up against me.
Deliver me from those who work evil;
from the bloodthirsty save me. (Psalm 59:1-2)

One of the things we learn from the psalms is the value of expressing our anguish—perhaps repeatedly. In many of the psalms for deliverance and protection, the psalmist goes on and on about the sins of the enemy, about all that has happened, about the evil deeds done. The psalmist embellishes and exaggerates, creating vivid images of the terrible straights he is in. He repeats himself so there is no doubt that he will be heard and believed. And throughout the psalm he proclaims his own righteousness and faithfulness and his love of God, picturing himself as all good while the enemy is all bad.

These psalms are similar to the grieving process in which healing occurs only when we tell our story over and over again. Repetition and exaggeration are helpful because the words make the situation real and because more people can hear the story with compassion. When something bad has happened, we want others to believe just how terrible it is. When we feel believed, we are reassured and begin to move from despair to hope, and from vengeance to compassion.

In the early 1980s I was living in California north of San Francisco when a trailside killer was loose in the surrounding hills. He had struck many times, usually attacking women or men hiking alone. I had hiked those trails alone for years, and suddenly authorities, family, and friends were telling me that I was not safe, that I should walk with a group, that I should abandon the hills.

I was enraged, not at my friends for their concern for my safety, but at this person who had murdered so many people and who was now restricting my freedom. How often I had turned to those hills for comfort and nurture. I took my troubles and my fears to those hills. I found God in those hills, and my strength was restored. Now "my" hills no longer belonged to God but to some evil force.

I talked about the unfairness, the injustice, the horror of what was happening to anyone who would listen. I hiked alone in angry defiance. I avidly read the newspaper as authorities followed clues. I wanted this man captured, imprisoned, executed.

One Sunday morning worship during silent prayer, I cried out my fury against this stranger. I began to go on and on with God as I had been going on and on with my friends. Suddenly something shifted. My heart seemed to split open, and I felt the pain and fear and illness of this unknown enemy. I imagined his alienation, his broken spirit, his fear, and his compulsion to murder. I found myself praying: "O my God, help him, help him. O my God, help him."

LOVE YOUR ENEMIES

When we have raged long enough, God softens our hearts. When we have cried out for vengeance, God opens us to compassion. When we are willing to start our prayers wherever our hearts are, God moves within us so that we become obedient to Jesus' command: "Love your enemies, and pray for those who persecute you."

This command was given by Jesus to show his followers a new way of living in the world. I believe the statement was meant to take his followers beyond their previous experience but not to negate the experience of hate. Jesus knew what was in people's hearts. He knew the old teachings. The psalms were Jesus' prayer book. Jesus tells us to pray for those who persecute us. He does not tell us not to feel angry. He does not tell us not to want vengeance. By telling us to love our enemies, Jesus is telling us not to remain in our pain and despair, not to get stuck in hatred. Jesus points us to the possibility of redeemed relationships with our sisters and brothers. He does not deny us the full experience of our hearts.

There might be times when we are ready to pray for our enemies with love and compassion. If that is true for you, offer a prayer of gratitude to God who is love, and pray that the one who has persecuted you will experience the love of God and know the hope God offers.

But if your heart is hardened against your enemy and you are filled with anger and despair, turn to God with your feelings of abandonment, your desire for vengeance, your need for protection and deliverance. Give voice to these prayers as long as you must. God will not leave you there. God will soften your heart and fill you with compassion. Jesus' words, "Pray for those who persecute you," are as much a promise as they are a command.

FOR REFLECTION AND DISCUSSION

1. Remember a time when your heart was softened toward an enemy. As you recall the situation, see if you can describe the process. What were the roles of others, of time, of circumstances? Where, when, and how did you experience God? What did you learn from that experience?

2. Remember an enemy toward whom your heart has softened. Recall the situation, the person's behavior, attitude, words. Look deep within yourself to explore the enemy within. What aspects of the other person are yours as well? How was that person a mirror for your own personality? See if you are willing to take your discoveries to God in prayer.

ACTIVITIES

1. Pick one of the following psalms to guide you in praying for enemies:

> Psalms for vengeance: 58, 83, 109, 137
>
> Psalms for deliverance: 4, 5, 13, 17, 22,
>   31, 35, 37, 57, 59, 69, 70, 120, 143
>
> Psalms for protection: 61, 64, 86, 91
>
> Psalm for a friend who betrayed you: 55

2. Write your own psalm of anger and fury. Remember to put yourself in God's presence as you write, knowing that by speaking the unspeakable clearly and specifically, you are turning the cry for justice over to God. Writing a psalm of vengeance is a profound act of faith.

3. If your heart is ready, enter into the following prayer.

Silence yourself and move into God's presence with words of gratitude and praise. Close your eyes and imagine your enemy at a good distance from you, yet close enough that you can see him or her. If you feel afraid imagine that Jesus is sitting with you, giving you courage and strength. Watch your adversary, recalling behavior, words, and attitudes that have distressed you. Then imagine both you and your enemy bathed in the love of God. Sit with this image as long as you are able, paying attention to any changes in the person or yourself. When you are ready let the image fade and rest for a moment while you continue to experience God's love. Close your prayer with words of thanksgiving for any grace that you received.

FIVE ❧ *The Process of Intercessory Prayer*

Not my will but yours.
—Luke 22:42

THE PROCESS OF INTERCESSORY PRAYER begins with God. God already loves us. God is already involved in our lives and the lives of those for whom we pray. God calls us into a network of relationships with God and all of creation. When we pray for others, we respond to God's call and become engaged with God and our sisters and brothers. Our prayer is also an expression of gratitude for God's ongoing presence in our lives.

Intercessory prayer is an exploration into our relationship with God and our relationship with our sisters and brothers.

We shall not cease from exploration
And the end of all of our exploring
Will be to arrive where we started
And know the place for the first time.[1]

God is the beginning and the destination in the process of intercessory prayer. God calls us. God is waiting for us. And when we meet God through prayer, we know God as we have never known God before. We are different. Our prayers are transformed by the journey.

Paul is an example of a man who was transformed through prayer. His prayer for the Ephesians, "May you know the hope to which he has called you," comes from a deep love and trust in God and a mature love for his sisters and brothers in Christ. Paul's

45

prayers reflect his long journey and his surrender to God. His prayers are open ended. They express no specific requests. Paul hopes; he does not wish.

We cannot expect our prayers to begin as Paul's ended. When we first respond to God's call to pray for others, we are filled with wishes. "Oh, God, I wish he had a better job." "I wish you would do something about my teenager. He doesn't listen to me." "I wish she would take better care of herself. Help her, God." We do not have a record of Paul's early prayers. I suspect they were much like ours. I imagine Paul wished before he surrendered into hope.

OBSTACLES TO PRAYER

Jesus, however, does give us a vision of the transformation that occurs in prayer. Like Paul's prayer for the Ephesians, Jesus' prayer in Gethsemane is the prayer of a man who knows and trusts God. He surrenders himself to God with the words, "Not my will but yours be done." But before he utters these words, he prays, "Father, if you are willing, remove this cup from me" (Luke 22:42). Before he surrenders, Jesus expresses his own desire.

This one verse of Scripture holds the process and the promise of intercessory prayer. Jesus teaches us to start with what is in our hearts. In time we will be led to surrender. If we have wishes, we call them out. If we are angry, we give it voice. If we don't know what we want, we speak our contradictions. When my mother was dying, I was confused. One moment I would pray for her to be healed, the next that she would be released. I would pray that God would give her courage to go on. I would pray for her to let go. My heart was in turmoil, so my prayers were in turmoil.

Confused prayers do not seem right to us. As our words and thoughts and feelings come forth all jumbled, we remember what we have read about prayer. Old teachings about how to pray float back into our minds and hearts. We compare ourselves to others and decide our prayers are not good enough. Often we decide not to pray but instead to read one more book about prayer. "I'll pray when I figure out how," we promise. Our need to "do it right" overshadows our longing to pray.

In a workshop on intercessory prayer, I invited the participants to introduce themselves to one another, then tell the person they had just met that they would pray for him or her during the day. They could also ask the person they met if he or she would pray for them. What resistance! "I don't know what the person needs." "I don't know how." "You haven't taught us yet." "What if I pray wrong?" Most of the people had come to hear about prayer. They did not know they had come to pray. With encouragement they began to pray from their resistance, from their confusion, and from their fear. Making the commitment to each other, then praying whatever was in their hearts, turned the workshop into a day of prayer.

"Dressing up for God" can be another obstacle to prayer. As children many of us were taught to put on our "Sunday best" to go to church. We polished our shoes, put shiny ribbons in our hair, and tried to monitor our behavior to match our outfits. As adults we might still be careful about how we dress for church. When this social custom is transferred to our inner lives, we become afraid to go to God in prayer because we are messy, rumpled, barefoot, or dirty. But going to God to share all parts of ourselves allows us to know God's unconditional love. Going to God exactly as we are gives us the freedom to pray at any time, in any mood, with all our thoughts and feelings. We do not need to be all cleaned up inside for God.

Neither do we have to clean up our words for God. Many of the spoken prayers we hear, or printed prayers we read, are poetic, filled with fine language, and so polished that we begin to feel that our inner prayers must match this eloquence. God does not care about grammar or vocabulary. God does not care if we stutter and grope for words. Our words might tumble over each other in our eagerness, or halt before our emptiness. Hearing a devout and experienced minister groping for words in a pastoral prayer, stopping, starting over, and pausing mid-sentence taught me to end the search for the perfect word or phrase. When we perform for God, we might miss what is in our hearts.

Sometimes our prayers seem selfish because we pray primarily from our own needs. A student once told me that when she received a call from her family with the news that her father was very ill and nearing death, she began to pray that he live long enough for her to reach him to say good-bye. She prayed continually as she made plane reservations, found someone to feed her cats, packed, and traveled to his bedside. When she got there, he was still alive but in such pain that every breath keeping him alive was agony. "My prayers were so self-centered," she told me years later. "I wasn't thinking of him. I focused only on myself and my desire to see him."

We often pray for others out of our own need. We pray that our spouse will be offered a particular job, not because he or she wants it but because we are tense with the reality of unemployment. We pray that our daughter's marriage will be healed, for we do not want divorce in the family, while she prays for the courage to leave her unfulfilling relationship. We pray for good weather before the family trip, although we know the farmers need rain.

We need not punish ourselves when we run into obstacles to prayer. Trying to do it right, thinking we have to dress up for God, struggling to find the perfect words, or focusing on selfish needs are all an integral part of our prayer life. They appear when we long to respond to God's call to relationship. They are a sign that we have been moved by the Spirit and have entered the process of prayer. Trying to anticipate and overcome every obstacle before we pray leaves God out of the process. When we begin prayer by allowing everything to pour out of our hearts, God will enter our hearts and prayers, and the obstacles we meet will be transformed.

PERSISTENT PRAYER

Once we begin the process of intercessory prayer, we are called to persistence. Moses pleaded not once but many times for God to have mercy on the people of Israel. The psalmist cried for justice over and over again. Jesus taught through his parable of the widow and the unjust judge (Luke 18:1-8) and the friend at midnight (Luke 11:5-8) that we are to persevere in our requests.

Persistence and perseverance do not mean mindless repetition. We do not simply duplicate the same prayer day after day. Rather, persistence allows our thoughts and feelings and desires to unfold. Persistence in prayer becomes a dynamic process in which God's grace is acting on us even as we pray. We find ourselves praying in new ways with different words, for surprising people, with unexpected requests. Persistence in prayer transforms our wishes into hopes and our own agendas into loving commitments to those for whom we pray.

St. Teresa of Avila likens those beginning and persevering in prayer to the silkworm, whose task in life is to eat leaves, chew, and spin.[2] As this pattern is repeated, new leaves are eaten and new strands spun, until the silkworm has spun itself into a cocoon. The cocoon, the container for transformation, would not be possible if the silkworm had not continued to eat and chew and spin.

TRANSFORMATION OF PRAYER

Transformation of our prayers is not as abrupt as the silkworm's shift from worm to chrysalis to butterfly. But St. Teresa teaches us that faithful practice of persistent prayer makes us available for God's transforming grace.

I often try to imagine the surprise of that little worm waking up one morning as a butterfly. It probably had no idea what was coming as it ate and chewed and spun. And like the worm, we have no idea what is coming as we persistently practice intercessory prayer. We might think we know where we are going. We might hope we will reach full maturity in the spiritual life. We might imagine others will draw to us and we will gather a following. We might think someone will invite us to write a book about prayer. We might believe we will become holy.

To arrive at a destination and know it for the first time is to be surprised. God enters our lives in new ways and our prayers change. Like an outgrown suit the way we used to pray no longer fits. Something we could not imagine has happened. The practice of intercessory prayer leads us away from the familiar into a realm where we are no longer in charge. Perseverance in prayer leads to surprises.

I don't like surprises. On my eighteenth birthday a group of friends gave me a surprise party. Two weeks before the day, a boy I liked a lot invited me to go to San Francisco to see the new movie *Around the World in 80 Days*. When I told him that date was my birthday, he seemed very surprised and said, "Then we will make it a very special time." I was so excited. That evening I wore a sophisticated black suit. I had red high heels and a purse to match. He came to get me, and on the way out of town he suggested we stop for a moment at a friend's house to retrieve something he had left there. The friend and his family were also good friends of mine, so when he said, "Why don't you come in too? I'm sure Tom's mom would love to see you," I went willingly. I wanted her to see how grown-up I looked.

We got to the door, pushed the bell, and waited only a few moments before they answered. I walked into a darkened living room, and all of a sudden there were twenty people laughing and yelling, "Surprise! Surprise!" Everyone was so pleased with themselves. They could tell from my face that I didn't have a clue. Tom's mother took me to a room where she had a pair of my jeans and a sweater that my mother had brought over. "I'm sure you'll be more comfortable in these," she said. "Everyone is dressed so casually."

I changed my clothes in a daze and returned to the front of the house. It was the summer before my friends and I were leaving for college. There were joke presents and great hilarity. Everyone had a wonderful time. I was confused and miserable. I was unable to make the transition from the evening I had planned to the evening I was in. I never caught up with myself. I missed my own birthday party.

I associate surprise with loss. I lost an election I was supposed to win. My father died suddenly of a heart attack when he was sixty, although he had no history of heart disease. A man I was dating and hoped to marry told me one evening over dinner that he had decided we were not a good match. I was thrown from a horse, and in one instant my summer turned from one of opportunity and adventure to months of slow and painful recuperation. These memories have kept me resistant to and wary of all surprises.

I am learning to change this attitude, for I understand that to avoid surprise is to resist God's grace. As a way of helping me shift my negative association with surprise, my spiritual director asked me to tell him about the good surprises I have experienced. I could only remember two. Now he has sent me in search of good surprises, not in my history but in the present moment: the surprise call from an old friend, the sudden shift in my body when I am dancing, the unexpected snow shower, the insight into Scripture that seems to come from nowhere, the stirring compassion for one who has betrayed me.

SURRENDER

Surprise is connected to surrender. Remember the silkworm? It had to "die" in the cocoon before it could be surprised by the transformation. We too must "die in our cocoons." We must surrender to God if our prayers are to be transformed.

Surrender is not a popular concept. It carries the images of defeat, withdrawal, powerlessness, and victimization. In a world that admires striving, getting ahead, and being in charge, surrender is equivalent to failure. But surrender is rich with possibilities if we are willing to look beyond the narrow interpretation.

Surrender is letting go and giving up the tension of holding on. Imagine a child swinging on a long rope over a clear pool. She clings tightly as she glides back and forth, back and forth, and suddenly she lets go and flies into the water below. Think of a time you were struggling with a problem, tense and worried with no solution in sight. Then you gave up and took a nap or took a walk or played ball with your child or baked a cake, and suddenly—the solution. Remember those delicious moments when you feel tensions of the day beginning to slide, your thoughts settling and your body relaxing, and you surrender into sleep.

Surrendering to God is difficult. In fact, I am not sure we can *do* it. Surrender is done to us. Trying to surrender is like trying to go to sleep. The harder we try, the more awake we become. We fall asleep when sleep overtakes us. We surrender to God when God overtakes us. When this happens we have arrived where we started, for God has been with us from our earliest moments in time.

The process of intercessory prayer begins with God and ends with God. We explore our hearts and offer in prayer for others whatever we find there. We explore the possibility of surrender and surprise. We examine our attitudes, our fears, and our resistance. As we search our hearts, we do not cease to pray for our sisters and brothers, for they are our prime concern. We persevere in our imperfect prayers—praying, praying, praying. We begin to notice that our prayers are slowly changing, our hearts are slowly opening. Then one day we discover we are truly praying that all people find the hope to which God has called them. We discover we are able to pray without a shred of doubt: "Your will be done." How and when this happens and what it will look like in your unique life is God's surprise.

FOR REFLECTION AND DISCUSSION

1. Reflect on the obstacles to prayer mentioned above: the need to do it right, dress up for God, find elegant words, or sort out your own needs from the needs of those for whom you pray. Which is most likely to keep you from intercessory prayer? Are there other things that keep you from praying?

2. What is your attitude about surprises? Remember the positive and negative reactions ones you have experienced. Begin to look for little surprises in your daily life.

ACTIVITIES

1. Make a list of all the wishes you have regarding other people. They might be kind or mean, large or small. Censor nothing. Take your list to God in prayer, saying, "God, these are my desires."

2. Remember a time when you experienced the joy of surrender. Think about the details of that experience. Remember how your body felt, what you were feeling, and what you were thinking. Allow yourself to reexperience that time of surrender in your imagination. As you do, let an image emerge that captures the joy that was there for you. Draw your image or describe it in words.

SIX ❧ *The Effects of Intercessory Prayer*

Ask, and it will be given you.
—*Luke 11:9*

SCRIPTURE TELLS US that our prayers will be answered. Faithful people everywhere pray for others, trusting that their prayers will have a beneficial effect. Questioning whether prayers have power is seen by some as evidence of a lack of faith, and a search for verification of the efficacy of prayers as an unfaithful act. But many people view doubts, questions, and experiments as an integral art of the faithful life. As they see it, searching for truth engages the mind, as well as the heart and soul. And in this modern age, in particular, science gives us knowledge to deepen our wisdom and our faith.

Among those fascinated by studies of the efficacy of prayer is Larry Dossey, M.D., whose books summarize the research that has been done.[1] Dr. Dossey offers his own insights into the implications of the research. Many experiments, which he describes, have been done with the ill to see how prayer affects healing.

One recent study by Dr. Randolph Byrd on the effect of prayer on heart patients was "designed according to rigid criteria, the kind usually used in clinical studies in medicine."[2] Three hundred ninety-three patients were studied. One hundred ninety-two patients had five to seven people praying for them daily. The remaining 201 patients received no prayers. The prayed-for patients had positive, significant differences in their healing.

Although this study received national attention, there were many criticisms because of the number of factors that were impossible to control. For this reason many scientists have turned to nonhuman studies to test the efficacy of prayer. Researcher Daniel J. Benor, M.D., discovered that at least 131 studies had been done prior to 1990.[3] The studies most helpful for our purpose are those conducted by the organization called Spindrift in Salem, Oregon.[4]

The Spindrift researchers tested the interaction of prayer with a simple biological system. They chose germinating seeds to see if prayer, and what kind of prayer, would positively affect the growing process. From many series of seed experiments, they concluded that prayer works. They also found that nondirected prayer was more effective on the sprouted seeds than directed prayer.

Directed prayer was defined as "prayer that attempted to influence the seeds toward a specific goal, image, or outcome that the pray-er had in mind." *Nondirected prayer* was defined as "an open-ended approach in which no specific outcome was held in the imagination."[5] In other words, the pray-er did "not attempt to tell the universe what to do."[6]

> An obvious question arises concerning nondirected prayer: If one does not pray for a specific result, how can one tell if the prayer is answered? Spindrift believes, on the basis of a large number of tests, that when a nondirected prayer is answered, the outcome is always in the direction of "what's best for the organism."[7]

These studies are helpful for our understanding of intercessory prayer, but we must be careful that they do not block our natural process of praying. We could read this information and begin to think, "Nondirected prayer? How am I supposed to do that? How can I be in prayer without an image? What should I do about the outcome I want? I probably can't do this right. Maybe I won't pray." The studies tell us that any form of prayer is beneficial. Do not allow the results to get in your way. Remember the process of prayer. The experiments simply confirm what faithful people throughout history have believed: praying for others makes a difference.

LOWERING THE THRESHOLD

More intriguing to me than whether prayer works is speculating on what actually happens in the organism or in the person for whom we pray. There might never be an answer from either science or faith, but philosopher Douglas Steere has an image that is helpful. He wrestles with the possibility that intercessory prayer could infringe upon the freedom of the people for whom we pray. He decides it does not because "the effect of our prayers for them would be at most to lower the threshold in the person prayed for and to make the besieging love of God . . . slightly more visible and more inviting."[8] People still have the freedom to "accept or reject the invitation that is being forever offered."[9]

Lowering the threshold is an interesting image. Imagine a wall with the besieging love of God on one side and the person we are praying for on the other. Our prayers do not bring God's love to the other, for God's love is always present and God is always waiting for people to respond. Our prayers do not force God to do anything to another. Our prayers lower the wall, so that people can experience what is already there. As the wall comes down, people might become more aware of God's love, more open to God's love, more willing to receive God's love. People for whom we pray have the choice to accept or reject God's presence in their lives.

God's invitation is always there for everybody. God does not withdraw, even if we have said no a thousand times. When others intercede for us, their prayers lower our resistance, help us to remember that God is always calling, and make more possible our acceptance of that call. God was calling the paralytic in the story in Mark's Gospel, but the paralyzed man needed the prayers of four friends in order to be able to accept the invitation. The friends' prayers through action lowered him into the presence of Jesus, where he could receive the gift of healing.

When I was awaiting minor surgery that required a general anesthetic, I asked many friends to pray for me. They knew the operation was scheduled for 11:00 A.M. At the appointed hour there was no movement to take me to surgery and no sign of the doctor. I was still lying in the preparation room. I asked my husband to read Psalm 30 aloud. I remembered my friends as the words swirled around me. I felt myself slide into a place of calm and gratitude. I felt held in love. When the nurse came for me an hour later, my blood pressure had dropped significantly, and I was ready, body and spirit, for the ordeal ahead. I believe prayer lowered my threshold and allowed God's grace to flood in.

More immediate is the experience of asking people to pray with me while I am writing this book. My hope has been to write a prayerful, not an academic, book about praying. Yet my active mind and my scholarly training keep pulling me to read one more study, get my Christology straight, and write in theological language. My feelings pull me away from prayer as I wonder if the book is good enough, whether anyone will read it (let alone like it), whether I will finish it on time.

I need the prayers of others to keep me writing with my heart centered on God. I don't know what people are praying for. I'm not sure how regularly they pray. I do know, as I sit in this mountain cabin praying and writing, I am not alone. Asking for the prayers has made a difference. I find it easier to let go of the thoughts that interfere and the feelings that pull me out of focus. I find it easier to turn back to God. I am more willing to be surprised by what I write. Asking for prayers has lowered my threshold and allowed God's creative energy to stir my heart.

BECOMING GOD-CENTERED

Formal experiments, stories of others, and our own experience tell us that intercessory prayer works. It works for the ones receiving the prayers, and it works *on* the one praying. "Intercession for another reveals its true nature in lowering the threshold to the divine entry in both the one who prays and the one who is prayed for."[10] Entering into the practice and the process of intercessory prayer transforms not only our praying but our lives.

Praying for others places God in the center of our existence. We turn toward God on behalf of others. Our attention becomes God-centered. Without prayer our concern for others turns outward to the world or inward to ourselves. Without God at the center, we become lost in the struggles of the world or lost in our own feelings about what we see.

So much is wrong in our society: young people dropping out of school, farmers losing their land, increased gang activity, political upheaval, famine, and disease. Looking at the world is important, but if our attention remains there, we can fall into despair, harden our hearts, or decide to look no more. When we turn toward God and take the people and the situations into prayer, we discover that we can see the horror and hold the hope of God's promise at the same time.

Sometimes when we look out into the world, we begin to focus on our own feelings and issues. We watch our children gain their independence and move away from us. We worry and fret and wonder if we have been good parents. We are besieged with negative campaigning by those running for political office. We judge and criticize and remember how it used to be. We chair a board meeting for an organization dedicated to peacemaking, and we hear the arguments, the competition, and the individual agendas. We begin to doubt our capabilities and believe we are not up to the task.

Paying attention to our thoughts and feelings is necessary, but to remain self-centered is to exclude God. Turning away from our own emotional concerns toward God in prayer restores a right relationship with God, ourselves, and our sisters and brothers. Intercessory prayer leads us toward obedience of the great commandment: "You shall love the Lord your God with all your heart, and with all your soul, and with all your strength, and with all your mind; and your neighbor as yourself" (Luke 10:27).

Intercessory prayer is about love. When we pray for others, our relationships are transformed from objective, fairly utilitarian

I/it relationships to intensely personal, mutual I/Thou relationships.[11] To see others as Thou draws us closer to them. We see ourselves reflected in them; we see God in them; we love them. We discover true compassion.

DISCOVERING COMPASSION

Compassion is often confused with feeling sorry for another, being moved to tears over another's experience, expressing deep concern about a situation in the world. But true compassion is deeper than that and demands an entirely different response.

> The word compassion is derived from the Latin words *pati* and *cum,* which together mean "to suffer with." Compassion asks us to go where it hurts, to enter into places of pain, to share in brokenness, fear, confusion, and anguish. Compassion challenges us to cry out with those in misery, to mourn with those who are lonely, to weep with those in tears. Compassion requires us to be weak with the weak, vulnerable with the vulnerable, and powerless with the powerless. Compassion means full immersion in the condition of being human.[12]

Intercessory prayer lowers our threshold to the divine entry. Intercessory prayer also lowers our threshold and allows our sisters and brothers in need to enter our hearts. Our prayers are no longer simply motivated by compassion. They become the very beat of the compassionate heart.[13]

Mark Twain's *The War Prayer* gives us a picture of people praying fervently but without compassion. In this vivid story a country is at war and all the young men are about to leave for the front. There is great excitement in the air, with eloquent speakers assuring victory, marching bands calling the crowds to patriotic fervor, and preachers evoking God's protection for the soldiers.

On a final Sunday—during worship services—one impassioned preacher is completing a long and poetic prayer for victory and the safe return of these brave young men. A stranger quietly moves to the front of the church and cries: "I come from the Throne, bearing a message from Almighty God!" With everyone's rapt attention, the newcomer goes on to proclaim that God has heard the preacher's prayers, as well as the unspoken prayers that lie beneath the plea for victory. He tells the people that he has been sent by God to put his heartfelt prayer into words.

"Listen!" he says. "Along with your prayer for victory, this too is your prayer."

> *Oh Lord our God,*
> *Help us to tear the enemy soldiers*
> *to bloody shreds with our shells;*
> *Help us to convert their smiling fields*
> *with the pale forms of their patriot dead;*
> *Help us to wring the hearts of their unoffending widows*
> *with unavailing griefs.*
> *For our sakes, who adore thee Lord,*
> *Blast their hopes,*
> *Blight their lives,*
> *Protract their bitter pilgrimage,*
> *Make heavy their steps,*
> *Water their way with their tears.*
> *We ask it, in the spirit of love,*
> *of Him who is the Source of Love,*
> *AMEN!*

And the stranger disappears as suddenly as he had arrived. Mark Twain ends his cautionary tale with the words:

> It was believed afterwards that the man was a lunatic, because there was no sense in what he said.[14]

Although the prayer that the stranger put into words sounds like one of the psalms of vengeance, there is a difference. Psalms of anger and revenge are offered consciously from a pain-filled heart. They are offered to God in the hope that God will bring justice and that the world, including the pray-er and the enemy, will be transformed. The people in Mark Twain's story remained unconscious of the fullness of their prayer. They looked only to their own desires and closed their eyes to the suffering of others. They were swept away with excitement and fear, but their hearts were hard. The stranger came to awaken their compassionate hearts. He failed.

True compassion brings us into solidarity with all of God's people. Solidarity not only connects us to others, it makes us one with all our sisters and brothers, including those on the opposite side of the battlefield. Compassion and solidarity are not easy. They are awakened in us slowly. As we pray for others, our prayers are gradually transformed, our hearts are softened, and our eyes are opened. Once opened we can never close our eyes again. We begin to see the world through God's eyes of love.

DEVELOPING PATIENCE

In addition to compassion and solidarity, those who practice intercessory prayer are brought to patience. Mark Twain's visitor from the throne of Almighty God was the picture of impatience. "Can't you see what you are doing?" he thundered. "Wake up! Wake up!" But the cocoon cannot be opened until the butterfly is ready. Hearts cannot be surrendered into compassion until people are prepared.

We live in an impatient world. Everyone is trying to get somewhere. Everyone is trying to leave somewhere behind. When a sudden snowstorm closes an airport, many people move into a frenzy. They yell at the airline personnel, pace, and drink. Their time schedule has been upset. Other people settle into the situation, getting out their paperwork or the book they have been waiting to read. They make a few phone calls so people will not worry. They chat with others and care for children of harried parents.

Patience is not passive waiting but active presence in the moment. Patience is trusting that all will be done in the fullness of time. As Julian of Norwich writes, "Sin is inevitable, but all shall be well, and all shall be well, and all manner of things shall be well."[15]

Intercessory prayer sometimes feels like being stuck in an airport during a snow storm. Our schedules are of no importance. Our impatience gets us nowhere. Our urgency produces no results. God seems not to care. But storms blow over and snow does melt. Change will happen, but not exactly when we want. Our task is to continue to pray while we are present to the moment and to the opportunities offered.

Often our waiting is much longer than the passing of the storm. Sometimes we pray for what might not happen in our lifetime. A Catholic laywoman, praying for and acting toward the ordination of women in the Catholic church, was asked by a reporter at a prayer vigil if she thought she would see women ordained in her lifetime. "Probably not," she replied. "Then why are you doing this?" the incredulous newsman asked. "I believe in this so strongly, what else is there to do?" she answered, with a light in her eyes. "My prayer and my action are a small and necessary part in this issue of justice. Women will be ordained into the priesthood. Sometime."

Patience leads us into the midst of the present moment. Patience leads us back into solidarity with others and deepens our compassion. When our hearts are open in the midst of life, we discover not only grief, struggle, and suffering. We discover laughter, love, and joy. Developing patience through intercessory prayer leads us toward a profound gratitude for the gifts that God has given us.

GROWING IN GRATITUDE

A friend told me recently how she remembered thinking many times throughout her twenties, "Is this all there is?" The phrase applied to her marriage and to her work. Although she was not unhappy, she was always seeking more, looking toward another day when. . . . She was impatient. She was waiting for the future to unfold today. Now in her fifties, she says the phrase has changed, and she finds herself thinking and even saying aloud, "This is *all* there is! *This* is all there is." She is filled with gratitude and wonder. "After thirty years," she exclaims, "I've learned to recognize God's presence in every single moment. There is no rush. This is all there is!"

Gratitude does not close us off from the suffering and struggles of the world. Gratitude offers us an experience of thanksgiving while we attend to the pains and needs of others. We recognize and feel God's love. Intercessory prayer transforms our worldview from either/or to both/and. We do not have to choose between struggle and love, pain and hope, despair and promise. Mother Julian said that sin is inevitable *and* all will be well. When gratitude fills our hearts, God feels very close. Our prayers of intercession are offered in a spirit of hope and with trust in God's promise to creation.

Compassion, solidarity, patience, and gratitude slowly fill our minds and hearts as we faithfully practice intercessory prayer. The gift of hope comes from these fruits of an active prayer life. We receive this gift as pray-ers. We give this gift to those for whom we pray. Hope was alive for me in the hospital preparing for surgery. Hope replaced wishful thinking in my fifty-year-old friend. Hope filled the heart of Julian of Norwich. Paul prayed that the Ephesians might know the hope to which God had called them.

PRAYING AND ACTING

Intercessory prayers are the expression of loving relationships. Paul told the faithful in Corinth that love is patient, love is kind. He told them that love bears all things, believes all things, hopes all things, and endures all things (1 Corinthians 13:4, 7). When this love motivates service in the world, our actions are filled with compassion, hope, and a deep respect for those we serve. With this love our actions become the very beat of the compassionate heart.

Sometimes we are called to action before we are called to prayer. We are hard at work before we recognize the gifts of intercessory prayer. When this occurs we are not out of order. We have simply entered the cyclical process of prayer and action at a different point. A committed life of service will lead us into intercessory prayer, just as a deep and faithful prayer life will lead us into action.

God calls us into relationship with God and with neighbor. Whether we respond to this call by prayer or by action is of little importance. Prayer and action go hand in hand. We cannot have one without the other. God calls us out of God's own need for us to be active participants in creation. Responding however we can lowers our thresholds and opens our hearts to God's transforming grace. To intercede for others through prayer and action immerses us in the process of conversion. It turns our lives around, and we will never be the same.

Paul gives us a glimpse of this conversion in his letter to the Romans when he describes the way to attain a new life in Christ:

> Do not lag in zeal, be ardent in spirit, serve the Lord. Rejoice in hope, be patient in suffering, persevere in prayer. Contribute to the needs of the saints; extend hospitality to strangers. Bless those who persecute you; bless and do not curse them. Rejoice with those who rejoice, weep with those who weep. Live in harmony with one another. . . . (Romans 12:11-16)

As we practice intercessory prayer, this promised life will reveal itself slowly. The change will not be sudden. It might be so slow that we do not realize what is taking place. But in God's own time, like the silkworm that became a butterfly, we will one day find ourselves surprisingly new.

FOR REFLECTION AND DISCUSSION

1. Talk with people about intercessory prayer experiences that worked. Discuss surprising results to intercessory prayer. Listen for unique ways God responds to prayer.

2. Sometimes people pass off special things that happen as coincidences rather than answers to prayers. William Temple,

archbishop of Canterbury, was once heard to say: "When I pray, coincidences happen, and when I don't, they don't." What is your understanding of coincidence and prayer?

3. Remember times when you have experienced true compassion and have entered into places of pain, sharing in brokenness, fear, and confusion. Reflect on how you arrived at that place of compassion and how you and others were affected by the experience. Reflect in the same manner on times when you have been treated with true compassion by another, when you were met as a Thou in a time of great need.

4. What is your rhythm of prayer and action? Where do you enter the process? Do you allow one to flow into the other? Do you tend to stay in prayer and resist action, or do you act and forget to pray?

ACTIVITIES

1. Be intentional about asking people to pray for you during a time of struggle or when you are engaged in a specific project. Pay attention to how it feels to be prayed for. Do you feel that your threshold has been lowered? What has flowed in?

2. Take inventory of your patience and impatience. What causes you to lose your patience? How does impatience feel? Can you remember times when you were truly patient? Notice your behavior and the behavior of others in times of waiting: supermarket lines, doctors' offices, traffic jams, meetings that begin late. What are some ways you could cultivate patience in your daily life?

3. Make a list of all the things, large and small, for which you are grateful. Write your own prayer of praise, thanksgiving, and gratitude. Practice experiencing this gratitude at the same time that you enter into struggle, brokenness, and pain. Pay attention to your tendency to see the world as either/or, and notice when you are able to experience both/and.

SEVEN ✒ *The Practice of Intercessory Prayer*

Withdraw to deserted places and pray.
—Luke 5:16

A STUDENT IN CALIFORNIA shared with me that he was not praying as much as he wished. He felt called to prayer but was unable to find the time to respond. When we explored his dilemma, he recognized his attachment to praying on a strip of deserted beach, which was forty-five minutes from his home. That spot was where he felt closest to God and where he felt his heart release in thanksgiving and praise. No wonder he could not find time to pray. The drive alone took an hour and a half!

When Jesus tells us to withdraw to deserted places to pray, we do not have to take his words literally. For many people there are no empty rooms available, let alone a silent stretch of shore. Jesus' words taken metaphorically point us to the intentional practice of withdrawing from the activities, interruptions, and noise of every-day life. The deserted place might be a quiet heart, an open mind, and a willing spirit. Jesus' words call us to a way of being, an inner attitude, rather than a physical place.

We can discover this inner attitude whenever we are willing to turn toward God. We do not need an extended period of time to open our hearts in prayer. Deserted places can be found in the few minutes in the car while we wait for a red light to change, or in the thirty-minute wait in the doctor's office, or every time we hear the shrill of an emergency vehicle and are reminded of sisters and brothers in need.

But in addition to these captured moments, we often long for more time to spend in prayer. When this longing surfaces we must examine our daily schedules and the patterns of our lives to discover a realistic period and length of time to be in prayer. Morning prayer might be right for many people; it might not be possible for you. A half an hour before lunch works well for some, while others prefer twenty minutes in the late afternoon, and others pick the time right before bed.

We might need to be creative to find a place for prayer. Some people are able to maintain a small altar in their home on which they place objects to remind them of the presence of God in their lives. Others find that an ordinary chair, turned to face a window or a painting or a candle in their home or office, can become a holy place for prayer. "Just turning my desk chair around to face the wall and lighting a candle creates my sacred space," a woman told me.

One man stops regularly in a neighborhood church for twenty minutes on his way home from work. Another uses his noon walk to be in prayer. An old spruce tree becomes a place of prayer for a retired physician, who sometimes simply goes to the spot where it grows and gazes at it, sits under it, or climbs high among its branches. An elementary school teacher places her prayer cushion in the back corner of the book room and goes there during morning recess to pray.

Intercessory prayer is one of many forms of prayer you will use during prayer time. Sometimes silence will seem more appropriate. Sometimes you will want to read Scripture or just talk nonstop to God about any and everything. At times praise and gratitude will arise in your heart. At other times a call for help will burst forth. God delights in any prayerful response to God's call to relationship. However, if you wish to make intercessory prayer a part of your prayer practice, the following suggestions might be helpful.

GENERAL INTERCESSION

A prayer of general intercession does not name names or ask for particulars. Rather, categories of people, some known and others unknown, are lifted into God's presence.

You may use the following prayer or personalize it, changing the way God is addressed, adding or changing the categories, or altering what you request. Play with the ideas and the wording until you have a general prayer of intercession that is your own.

> *Gracious God, I pray . . .*
> > *for all those I love . . .*
> > *for all who are hard to pray for . . .*
> > *for all who are ill . . .*
> > *for all who grieve . . .*
> > *for all who have been forgotten . . .*
> *May they find comfort in your loving presence.*
> *Amen.*

INTERCESSION FOR SPECIFIC PEOPLE

When your prayer of intercession is for one person and you wish to devote all your prayer to him or her, begin with simple words of invocation, gratitude, or a request for guidance. Then in your mind's eye, visualize the person for whom you are praying. See the person as clearly as possible, both in motion and at rest. Allow memories of this person to come into your consciousness. If you have a specific request for this person, speak the words aloud or in your heart: "Dear God, give her courage." "Please God, let him know he is loved."

If you have no particular words of supplication, you might envision the person held in God's hands, surrounded with light, in the company of Jesus, or receiving God's blessing. Allow the image to take its own shape, and allow it to move from your mind to your heart. Then simply sit, moving into a receptive silence, drawing yourself gently back to the prayer if your attention begins to wander. When your time is up, slowly release the image of the person for whom you were praying, and close with a few words of thanksgiving.

When the prayer of intercession is for more than one person, the above prayer can be used in abbreviated form. If you have a number of people for whom you wish to pray, a notebook of intercessory prayer can be useful. Use the notebook to keep a list of people for whom you wish to pray. You can include photographs or mementos along with the names. Some people might be permanently in your book. Others might be added as their particular needs come to your attention and then removed as their situations change.

To pray for the people in your notebook you might use the phrase "God, I commend to you . . ." or "God, may . . . know your hope." Slowly and prayerfully repeat the sentence as you attend to each person. Images and memories will surface spontaneously, as will special requests. Honor these words and feelings and gently move on until you have named each person for whom you wish to pray. End with a brief prayer of thanksgiving.

You might not wish to practice these longer forms of intercessory prayer daily. One day a week set aside for praying for others might balance your daily prayers of reading, confession, silence, and praise. One day a month might be appropriate—or pray whenever you are so moved. The old saying "Pray as you can, not as you can't" is a helpful reminder as you organize your prayer life.

PRAYERS FOR THOSE WHO HAVE DIED

Many religious traditions do not regularly pray for the dead. Except at funerals and memorial services, and on select occasions such as All Saints Day or Memorial Day, those who have died are absent from our prayers. But they are not absent from our hearts. An anniversary day arrives, a song triggers a memory, an image surfaces in a dream, you catch a glimpse of your father's smile in your daughter's face. At these moments we might say a prayer for those who are gone but not forgotten.

Prayers for those who have died can be verbal prayers of thanksgiving for the gifts loved ones brought to our lives. They can be silent prayers for the everlasting peace of departed souls. They can be tearful prayers as we express our grief over unfinished issues, untimely death, loss, and abandonment. They can be action prayers, such as lighting a candle on the eve of a death anniversary, telling stories about the deceased, looking at old photographs, tending a grave.

We do not need to understand death to pray for those who have died. Neither do we need to be clear about our belief in the resurrection, life after death, heaven, hell, or eternity. Whatever our faith, death remains a mystery. Whatever our desire, memories arise to invite us into continuing relationships with the dead.

As in other forms of intercessory prayer, we cannot know how our prayers affect the soul of the one who is gone. But Thomas Moore speaks about the effect such prayers have on our own souls: "Fostering our relationships to the dead gives the soul its nourishment of eternity, melancholy, mystery, and the kind of relatedness that is not literally of this world."[1] Moore continues by inviting us to new possibilities: "In our individual lives, deep religious sensibility could arise from simple ways of remembering departed relatives and friends."[2]

If praying for those who have died is an unfamiliar intercession, the Catholic eucharist can provide a model of general intercession. Every time eucharist is celebrated, a prayer is offered for those who have gone before. The wording of these prayers helps all Christians find ways to express their prayers for departed loved ones.

> Remember our brothers and sisters who have gone to their rest in the hope of rising again. Bring them and all the departed into the light of your presence.[3]

> Remember those who have died in the peace of Christ and all the dead whose faith is known to You alone.[4]

COMPASSIONATE OBSERVER

The prayer of the compassionate observer is the prayer offered in the midst of a situation where it becomes apparent that God's help is needed. When I hear my husband arguing with our younger son, when voices rise and tears are close, I offer a prayer that they utter words not too hurtful and that they remain in dialogue until they find reconciliation. In a committee meeting when business and productivity are stalled, when personalities get stuck, a prayer for wisdom, patience, and the ability to untangle the issues might be offered. Many people in a congregation offer a brief prayer for the minister before the sermon begins. These are intercessory prayers of compassionate observers.

Compassionate observers are witnesses who recognize the need for prayer. The discipline of compassionate observers is to stay intimately connected to what is going on while not becoming involved. Compassionate observers are not detached; they are present to the people, to the struggle, and to God. When people become compassionate observers, they see, hear, and feel the situation in all its complexity and simply invite God's love and wisdom to touch the hearts of all participants.

PRAYERS FOR THE WORLD

The suffering, pain, and hunger of the people of the world can overwhelm us and leave us hopeless and despairing. Images cry out to us from Bosnia, Haiti, India, and our inner cities. Because there is so much suffering about which we can do little, we often close out the images, harden our hearts, and attend to the trials and delights of our own immediate lives. We forget that we can attend to the struggles of the world through prayer.

We can make events in the world part of our intercessory prayer life in the same way that we include individuals: name the situation or the location prayerfully, imagine the country or the people surrounded by light, or imagine our struggling world held lovingly in God's hands. For a longer prayer of intercession for the world, the following meditation or a similar one of your own design could be used.

Pick a situation in the world that is particularly troubling to you or touches your heart in a special way. You can choose the hungry of the world, people living with AIDS, people displaced by political upheaval, places touched by natural disaster. You can begin with a particular situation or a general category.

When you have decided on the focus of your prayer, settle yourself comfortably and take a few minutes to pay attention to your body . . . then your feelings . . . and finally your mind. Acknowledge how you are feeling and what you are thinking. Then turn your attention to God. Offer a brief prayer of invocation or thanksgiving or petition. Take a few deep breaths and quiet yourself. Then sit for a moment, experiencing the love that God brings into your heart.

In your mind's eye begin to visualize particular situations or locations that hold the struggle for which you have decided to pray. Open your heart to the images that begin to form, feeling the feelings that emerge. Feel God's presence with you and with the situations you are visualizing. Allow your imagination to take you around the world, to different continents, visualizing this form of struggle in as many ways as possible. Then bring your imagination back to your own country, acknowledging this suffering closer to home. Look to the major cities . . . the suburbs . . . the rural areas of our nation.

Imagine now this suffering in your own city or town. Imagine where this particular struggle is occurring in your churches, your schools, your neighborhood. Look closely and honestly to see if this struggle is occurring in your own family or within your own heart. Sit quietly in prayerful reflection with what you are discovering. If you find the growing awareness troubling, you might wish to invite Jesus to be with you as you pray.

After examining your own situation and the struggle as it manifests in areas close to home, move outward from your own location, seeing briefly again the situation throughout the world. In your imagination move far enough so that you can visualize the world as the astronauts see it from space. As you gaze upon the world, allow a prayer to form in your heart. It might be silent. It might be composed of images. It might consist of words. Sit quietly, offering this prayer to God. Stay in prayer as long as you wish.

When your prayer is ended, take a few minutes to allow the images to fade. Slowly bring your attention back to your immediate location, noticing sounds around you. Feel your body moving, stretching. Open your eyes. Offer a closing prayer.

PRAYERS FOR OUR LEADERS

> First of all, then, I urge that supplications, prayers, intercessions, and thanksgiving be made for everyone, for kings and all who are in high positions, so that we may lead a quiet and peaceable life in all godliness and dignity. (1 Timothy 2:1-2)

People in authority are in need of our prayers. We can pray for our leaders as part of our general intercession or for specific leaders in times of struggle, warfare, and calamity. Local, national, and world leaders are making daily decisions that affect the peace and dignity of all our lives. They are the ones who might help to realize God's kingdom on earth. They should not have to carry this awesome responsibility alone.

EARTH PRAYERS

Earth prayers are offered for the healing of the planet and for healing the human-earth relationship. Elizabeth Roberts and Elias Amidon have collected 365 prayers, poems, and invocations for honoring the earth in their book *Earth Prayers*.[5] In the introduction they acknowledge that we must act if we are to save the earth, but they also recognize that "the healing of our relationship with this planet ultimately needs to emerge from our hearts and our spirits."[6] They invite the reader to practice earth prayer as a way of connecting to the earth and to others across time, distance, and traditions who pray for the healing of the planet.

> The beauty of Earth Prayer is that it reminds us that we are not alone in this task. In forest clearings, beneath star-filled skies, in cathedrals, and before the hearth, men and women have always given voice to this impulse. In these prayers of the earth we join our voice with theirs to call forth the healing that is so needed.[7]

Prayers for the earth can be deepened when we use our bodies in the practice of intercessory prayer. After you have read or spoken a prayer, stand comfortably with your feet about a foot apart and relax your knees. Hold your hands together in front of your heart and cup them slightly as if you were holding the whole earth in your hands. Then slowly raise your hands above your head, extending your arms. Pause in that position, symbolizing the offering of the whole planet to God for healing. Gently bring your arms back down to your sides as if you were making angels in the snow. Repeat this body prayer for the earth three times.

PRAYER PARTNERS

Just as Jesus taught us to pray in private (Matthew 6:6), he also assured us, "For where two or three are gathered in my name, I am there among them" (Matthew 18:20). The practice of intercessory prayer expands because we uphold one another when we join with others to call upon God to hear our concerns. Any of the above suggestions could be modified to be used in small groups or with larger gatherings. In addition, there are forms of intercessory prayer that can only be done in community.

A prayer partner is helpful in the practice of any form of prayer, for we make an appointment with another person as well as with God. When two hold us accountable, we are more likely to show up! Some partners meet daily or weekly to pray. Others make a commitment to pray at the same time but do not physically come together.

Intercessory prayer partners make the commitment to pray regularly for each other. Two friends can become intercessory prayer partners, or members of a congregation can be randomly paired. Prayer partners can also be arranged for a particular purpose, such as a youth group planning a mission trip. Rather than praying a general intercession, each adult who wishes to participate draws the name of a young person and begins their prayers for the individual and the group during the months of preparation, praying also during the trip itself. The identity of who is praying for whom can be shared or can be held in private. If revealed the young people can in turn pray for their partners. If held in private, the youth group can pray for the whole congregation, which is supporting them in their mission work in the world.

PRAYER CHAINS

When particular needs arise within a congregation and prayers are requested, a prayer chain is a helpful tool to have in place. A prayer chain is like a telephone tree, where one person makes as many as three initial calls, and each contact calls up to three others, and so on, until all members who wish to take part have been notified.

The person who is requesting prayer decides how much information should be given and whether particular prayers are desired. A person must be free to request prayers for reconciliation for the family without giving details about the struggle. Prayers for healing might be requested without revealing the nature of the illness.

Congregations are sometimes wary of prayer chains, for they find that people use the information for gossip rather than for prayer. When we know a family is in trouble, or a friend is sick, curiosity can easily take the place of compassion and prayer. Congregational leaders can address these concerns as the people are educated about the sacred responsibility of intercessory prayer.

INTERCESSION DURING WORSHIP

Most Sunday worship services have a time for intercessory prayer. In the liturgical churches, the prayer is called the Great Intercession or the Prayer of the Faithful. In nonliturgical churches, the prayer time is often called the prayers of the people, sharing of joys and concerns, or the pastoral prayer. Intercession during corporate worship is an opportunity for all members of the congregation to participate in praying for others. Regular intercession also teaches people about carrying this prayer form into their lives. An excellent resource for building a life of corporate intercessory prayer is Walter C. Huffman's *Prayer of the Faithful*.[8]

A SERVICE OF INTERCESSORY PRAYER

A special service dedicated to intercessory prayer brings people together to ask God to be with brothers and sisters in need. The service could be held monthly, quarterly, or when the need arises in the community or the world. The following order of worship might be helpful to those who wish to organize and lead a service of intercessory prayer.

- Call to Worship
- Scripture Reading
- Musical Reflection
- Prayers of the People
   for individuals
   for situations
   for creation
- Silent Prayer
- Lord's Prayer
- Benediction

The service uses Scripture readings and music to lead people into a prayerful place where their hearts are open in compassion. Any of the Scripture references in this book would be appropriate, or choose another that you believe would lead people into the presence of God. Reading the Scripture in the style of *Lectio Divina* (Sacred Reading) can assist people in their interior movement.

In *Lectio Divina* a passage is read four times, with a full minute's pause between readings. The intent of each reading is different. During the first reading worshipers simply hear the words. The second reading is for thinking about the words. Listeners bring to mind what they know about the passage. The third reading allows listeners to respond to the passage in prayer. They talk to God about what they have heard and how they feel about it. In the fourth reading worshipers hear the word of God with their hearts. *Read, reflect, respond,* and *rest* are words that recall the four movements of *Lectio Divina.*

The musical reflection is designed to help participants continue their inward journey. If musicians are not available to play during the service, well-chosen music on tape or compact disc is appropriate. Choose words and music to encourage participants to express aloud their concerns for individuals; for particular situations in the local community, the nation, or the world; and for all of creation. These spoken concerns are the heart of the prayer service.

Each prayer might be followed by a congregational response, such as "Lord, hear our prayer" or "For this I pray to the Lord." Between each category of intercessory prayer, the congregation could sing a brief response, such as

> *Come, God of mercy,*
> *Send us your Spirit,*
> *Renew the face of the earth!*[9]

The leader of the service might wish to offer a spoken prayer that includes the concerns the community has expressed, followed by five to eight minutes of individual silent prayer (during which each person prays as the Spirit leads). The silence is ended as all pray the Lord's Prayer together, followed by the benediction.

FOR REFLECTION AND DISCUSSION

As you read through the many suggestions for intercessory prayer, which ones touched your heart and made you think, "That is one I could practice!"? Which ones did not appeal to you at all? (Some will naturally be more your style than others.) Then pay attention to your inner dialogue, listening for words and phrases that keep you from practicing the prayers you are drawn to. Interior statements that could get in your way might be: "That one is too hard"; "I don't have time for that one"; "I'll never get that one right"; or "I'm too inexperienced (or too advanced) for that one."

ACTIVITIES

1. Write your own prayer of general intercession. Keep it in a place you often attend to, such as your daily calendar, your address book, or the front of your Bible. Pray your general intercession every time you see it.

2. Begin your own notebook of intercessory prayer. Be creative in what you include.

3. Write your own earth prayer, similar to the longer prayer of intercession for the world found on page 72–73. Choose one aspect of the earth for which you have special concern, and then pray for that concern globally and locally.

4. Find some other people you believe might be interested in an intercessory prayer ministry. Meet together to decide with which of the community practices you might begin. Some groups begin by selecting prayer partners. Then, as the ministry grows, they share it with a larger community through a service of intercessory prayer. Others begin with the service as a way to interest people in regular intercessory prayer.

Notes

ONE: **The Theology of Intercessory Prayer**

1. Harold S. Kushner, *When Bad Things Happen to Good People* (New York: Schocken Books, 1981).

2. From the video *Human Suffering and the Power of God: Rabbi Harold S. Kushner Interviewed by Dr. John Cobb* (Claremont: The Center for Process Studies, 1984).

3. Walter Wink, *Engaging the Powers: Discernment and Resistance in a World of Domination* (Minneapolis: Fortress Press, 1992).

4. Ibid., 11.

5. Ibid.

6. Ibid., 298.

7. Ibid., 299.

8. Ibid., 303.

9. "Immortal, Invisible, God Only Wise," *The Presbyterian Hymnal* (Louisville: Westminster/John Knox Press, 1990), 263.

10. Wink, 299.

11. Douglas V. Steere, "Intercession: Caring for Souls," *Weavings: A Journal of the Christian Spiritual Life,* Volume IV, Number 2 (March/April 1989): 20.

TWO: **Human Responsibility**

1. Virginia Ramey Mollenkott, *Godding: Human Responsibility and the Bible* (New York: Crossroad, 1987), 6–9.

2. Geffrey B. Kelly, ed., *Karl Rahner: Theologian of the Graced Search for Meaning* (Minneapolis: Fortress Press, 1992), 176.

3. Dietrich Bonhoeffer, *Letters and Papers from Prison* (New York: The MacMillan Company, 1972), 347–48.

4. Ibid., 348.

5. Ibid.

6. Theodore W. Jennings, Jr., "Prayer: The Call for God," *The Christian Century*, Volume XCVIII, Number 13 (April 15, 1981): 412.

7. John Selby Spong, *Honest Prayer* (New York: The Seabury Press, 1973), 67.

8. Elizabeth Roberts and Elias Amidon, eds., *Earth Prayers from around the World* (San Francisco: HarperSanFrancisco, 1991), 367.

THREE: **Gospel Stories of Intercession**

1. Sibyl Harton, *The Practice of Intercession* (London and Oxford: A. R. Mowbray & Company, 1939), 21.

2. Ibid., 23.

3. See also 2 Corinthians 1:11; Ephesians 6:19; Philippians 1:19; Colossians 4:2; 1 Thessalonians 5:25.

4. Harton, 27.

5. Charles F. Whiston, "Intercession," *Review and Expositor: A Baptist Theological Journal,* Volume LXXI, Number 3 (Summer 1974): 320.

6. Flora Slosson Wuellner, *Heart of Healing, Heart of Light* (Nashville: The Upper Room, 1992), 91.

FOUR: **Intercession for Enemies**

1. Dietrich Bonhoeffer, *Psalms: The Prayer Book of the Bible* (Minneapolis: Augsburg Publishing House, 1970), 56–60.

FIVE: **The Process of Intercessory Prayer**

1. T. S. Eliot, "The Four Quartets," *The Complete Poems and Plays: 1909–1950* (New York: Harcourt, Brace, and World, 1952), 145.

2. Teresa of Avila, *The Interior Castle,* translated by Kieran Kavanaugh, B.C.D., and Otilio Rodriquez, O.C.D., (New York: Paulist Press, 1979).

SIX: **The Effects of Intercessory Prayer**

1. Larry Dossey, M.D., *Healing Words: The Power of Prayer and the Practice of Medicine* (San Francisco: HarperSanFrancisco, 1993).

2. Ibid., 180.

3. Ibid., 189.

4. Larry Dossey, *Recovering the Soul: A Scientific and Spiritual Search* (New York: Bantam Books, 1989), 54–62.

5. Ibid., 68.

6. Dossey, *Recovering the Soul,* 54–62.

7. Dossey, *Healing Words,* 98.

8. Douglas V. Steere, "Intercession: Caring for Souls," *Weavings: A Journal of the Christian Spiritual Life,* Volume IV, Number 2 (March/April 1989): 19.

9. Ibid., 20.

10. Ibid., 23.

11. Martin Buber, *I and Thou,* translated by Walter Kaufman (New York: Scribner, 1970).

12. Donald P. McNeill, Douglas A. Morrison, and Henri J. M. Nouwen, *Compassion: A Reflection on the Christian Life* (Garden City, N.Y.: Doubleday and Company, 1982), 4.

13. Ibid., 109.

14. Mark Twain, *The War Prayer* (New York: Harper and Row, 1966), 35.

15. Julian of Norwich, *Revelations of Divine Love,* translated by Clifton Wolters (London: Penguin Books, 1966), 35.

SEVEN: **The Practice of Intercessory Prayer**

1. Thomas Moore, *Soul Mates: Honoring the Mysteries of Love and Relationship* (New York: Harper Collins Publishers, 1994), 201.

2. Ibid., 203.

3. Eucharistic Prayer II, *The Roman Missal,* 1969.

4. Eucharistic Prayer IV, *The Roman Missal,* 1969.

5. Elizabeth Roberts and Elias Amidon, eds., *Earth Prayers* (San Francisco: HarperSanFrancisco, 1991).

6. Ibid., xix.

7. Ibid., xxiv.

8. Walter C. Huffman, *Prayer of the Faithful: Understanding and Creatively Leading Corporate Intercessory Prayer* (Minneapolis: Augsburg Fortress, 1992).

9. David Haas, "Send Us Your Spirit," *Gather: A Book of Song* (Chicago: G.I.A. Publications, 1988).

Further Reading

Barry, William A., S.J. *God and You: Prayer As Personal Relationship*. New York: Paulist Press, 1987.

Brueggemann, Walter. *The Message of the Psalms*. Minneapolis: Augsburg Publishing House, 1984.

Dossey, Larry, M.D. *Healing Words: The Power of Prayer and the Practice of Medicine*. San Francisco: HarperSanFrancisco, 1993.

Froehle, Virginia Ann, R.S.M. *Called into Her Presence: Praying with Feminine Images of God*. Notre Dame: Ave Maria Press, 1986.

Hall, Thelma. *Too Deep for Words: Rediscovering Lectio Divina*. New York: Paulist Press, 1988.

Huffman, Walter C. *Prayer of the Faithful: Understanding and Creatively Leading Corporate Intercessory Prayer*. Minneapolis: Augsburg Fortress, 1992.

Keating, Thomas. *Intimacy with God*. New York: Crossroad, 1994.

Kushner, Harold S. *When Bad Things Happen to Good People*. New York: Schocken Books, 1981.

Leech, Kenneth. *True Prayer*. San Francisco: Harper and Row, 1980.

Mollenkott, Virginia Ramey. *Godding: Human Responsibility and the Bible*. New York: Crossroad, 1987.

Moore, Thomas. *Care of the Soul.* New York: Harper Collins Publishers, 1992.

Nouwen, Henri J. M. *Reaching Out: The Three Movements of the Spiritual Life.* Garden City, N.Y.: Doubleday and Company, 1975.

Rupp, Joyce, O.S.M. *Praying Our Goodbyes.* Notre Dame: Ave Maria Press, 1988.

Wiederkehr, Macrina. *A Tree Full of Angels: Seeing the Holy in the Ordinary.* San Francisco: HarperSanFrancisco, 1988.

Wink, Walter. *Engaging the Powers: Discernment and Resistance in a World of Domination.* Minneapolis: Fortress Press, 1992.

Wuellner, Flora Slosson. *Prayer, Stress, and Our Inner Wounds.* Nashville: The Upper Room, 1985.